*Homilies on the "B" Cycle of Readings
for Sundays and Holy Days*

*"They recounted what had happened on the road
and how they had come to know him
in the breaking of the bread."*
(Lk 24:35)

BREAKING THE BREAD

Homilies on the "B" Cycle of Readings for Sundays and Holy Days

by
Charles E. Miller, C.M.
and
Oscar J. Miller, C.M.

alba house
A DIVISION OF THE SOCIETY OF ST. PAUL
STATEN ISLAND, NEW YORK 10314

Library of Congress Cataloging in Publication Data

Miller, Charles Edward, 1929-
    Breaking the bread.

    1. Catholic Church--Sermons.   2. Sermons, American.   I. Miller, Oscar J., 1913- II. Roebert, Michael M.   III.   Title.
BX1756.A2M56   252'.02   72-6155
ISBN 0-8189-0254-X

Imprimi Potest:
    Joseph S. Falanga, C.M.
    Vice Provincial, Los Angeles Vice Province

Nihil Obstat:
    John A. Grindel, C.M.
    Censor Deputatus

Imprimatur:
    +Timothy Manning
    Archbishop of Los Angeles
    March 25, 1972

The imprimi potest, nihil obstat and imprimatur are official declarations that a book or pamphlet is free of doctrinal or moral error. No implication is contained therein that those who have granted the imprimi potest, nihil obstat and imprimatur agree with the contents, opinions or statements expressed.

Copyright 1972 by the Society of St. Paul,
2187 Victory Blvd., Staten Island, New York 10314.

Designed, printed and bound by the Fathers and Brothers of the Society of St. Paul, 2187 Victory Blvd., Staten Island, N. Y. 10314 as part of their communications apostolate.

TABLE OF CONTENTS

Introduction ix
To The Preacher ix

1. First Sunday of Advent /
   A Second Christmas 1
2. Solemnity of the Immaculate Conception /
   Follow the Leader 4
3. Second Sunday of Advent /
   Beginning and End 6
4. Third Sunday of Advent /
   Do You Recognize Him? 10
5. Fourth Sunday of Advent /
   God's Christmas Preparations 14
6. Christmas Eve /
   A Change Is Made 17
7. Christmas Day /
   The Birth of Hope 21
9. Feast of the Holy Family /
   Mission: Impossible 24
10. Solemnity of Mary—New Year's Day /
    Renewal 27
11. Solemnity of the Epiphany /
    Equality of Man Before His Creator 30
12. The Baptism of Our Lord /
    Baptism and Humility 34
13. Second Sunday of the Year /
    Christ and His People 37
14. Third Sunday of the Year /
    Faith and Repentance 41
15. Fourth Sunday of the Year /
    Jesus, Lord and Savior 45
16. Fifth Sunday of the Year /
    Happily Forever After 49
17. Sixth Sunday of the Year /
    A People Set Apart 53

BREAKING THE BREAD

18. Seventh Sunday of the Year /
    Words of Forgiveness Still 57
19. Eighth Sunday of the Year /
    The Joy of Christians 61
20. Ninth Sunday of the Year /
    "I Don't Go to Church Any More" 65
21. First Sunday of Lent /
    The Christian Rainbow 69
22. Second Sunday of Lent /
    A Hint of Glory 73
23. Third Sunday of Lent /
    True Worship 77
24. Fourth Sunday of Lent /
    God So Loved the World 81
25. Fifth Sunday of Lent /
    A Law of Life 85
26. Passion Sunday /
    Cheers and Boos 88
27. Easter Sunday /
    Superstar! 91
28. Second Sunday of Easter /
    Faith Power Through Forgiveness 94
29. Third Sunday of Easter /
    The Least Likely is the Best Bet 97
30. Fourth Sunday of Easter /
    Invest in This Stock 100
31. Fifth Sunday of Easter /
    How to Trim Your Pride 103
32. Sixth Sunday of Easter /
    Oh Yes, He's a Personal Friend of Mine 106
33. Solemnity of the Ascension /
    The Flower of the Resurrection 109

Contents

34. Seventh Sunday of Easter /
    Jump, I'll Catch You   112
35. Pentecost Sunday /
    The Gift of Wisdom   115
36. Trinity Sunday /
    It's All Very Personal   118
37. Solemnity of Corpus Christi /
    "I Need a Cross"   122
38. Tenth Sunday of the Year /
    A Household Divided   125
39. Eleventh Sunday of the Year /
    A Growing Organism   127
40. Twelfth Sunday of the Year /
    Storms and Trust   130
41. Thirteenth Sunday of the Year /
    God Has Time for People   133
42. Fourteenth Sunday of the Year /
    A Prophet Without Honor?   137
43. Fifteenth Sunday of the Year /
    Change and Permanence   141
44. Sixteenth Sunday of the Year /
    Come and Rest   145
45. Seventeenth Sunday of the Year /
    Signs and the Eucharist   149
46. Eighteenth Sunday of the Year /
    Faith Comes From a Hearty Appetite   153
47. Nineteenth Sunday of the Year /
    Food for Traveling   156
48. Solemnity of the Assumption /
    Abundant Life   159
49. Twentieth Sunday of the Year /
    It's Wise to Eat   162

BREAKING THE BREAD

50. Twenty-First Sunday of the Year /
    Will You Stay? 165
51. Twenty-Second Sunday of the Year /
    Of Lips and Hearts 168
52. Twenty-Third Sunday of the Year /
    To Hear and to Speak 171
53. Twenty-Fourth Sunday of the Year /
    Make Up Your Mind 174
54. Twenty-Fifth Sunday of the Year /
    People Are Precious 177
55. Twenty-Sixth Sunday of the Year /
    Starfish and Christians 181
56. Twenty-Seventh Sunday of the Year /
    God's Idea of a Love Story 184
57. Twenty-Eighth Sunday of the Year /
    Happiness and the Eye of a Needle 187
58. Twenty-Ninth Sunday of the Year /
    The Servant and His Servants 191
59. Thirtieth Sunday of the Year /
    Faith and Thanksgiving 194
60. Solemnity of All Saints /
    The Saints Go Marching Out? 198
61. Thirty-First Sunday of the Year /
    Heart Speaks to Heart 201
62. Thirty-Second Sunday of the Year /
    The Widow's Mite 204
63. Thirty-Third Sunday of the Year /
    Life After Death: That's Progress 208
64. Solemnity of Christ the King /
    The King and His Nobles 211

Introduction

For this third time we are happy to provide a word of introduction to this volume entitled, *Breaking the Bread,* a companion to the two previous works from the same authorship. This completes the comments on the Sunday readings for the A, B and C cycles. The obvious success of the two previous volumes argues to the merits of this.

Our own recommendation at this juncture is that the volume should be used by the priests primarily as one of meditation. It is only in the measure in which these thoughts have become part of the soul of the priest that he can convincingly proclaim them to his congregation.

The hearts of the disciples on the road to Emmaus were aglow as the Lord companioned them, unknowingly, on the way. Behind the sequence of these pages may you follow Him toward the mystery of His revelation.

+ Timothy Manning
Archbishop of Los Angeles

To The Preacher

Pope Paul in his first encyclical, *Ecclesiam Suam,* stated that "preaching is the primary apostolate of the priest." That statement was re-asserted by Vatican II in its Decree on

BREAKING THE BREAD

the Ministry and Life of Priests: "Priests, as co-workers with their bishops, have the primary duty of proclaiming the word of God to all" (4). In our times the homily, whereby the priest preeminently fulfills his office as preacher, is regaining its rightful place as an integral part of the Mass.

This book, dedicated to the ministry of preaching, is called *Breaking the Bread*. The episode of the disciples on their way to Emmaus who came to know Jesus in the breaking of the bread was constructed by the evangelist in such a way as to make his readers think of both the liturgy of the word and the liturgy of the Eucharist. And quite rightly so, for early in the history of the Church the expression, "breaking the bread," came to be applied to the entire Mass (cf. Ac 2:24). The Mass contains both sacrament and word. The people are to be nourished with both the bread of the Eucharist and the bread of God's word in the scriptures and the homily. The challenge of today's preaching is to give people the solid food of God's word and to make that food as palatable as possible. In this connection Pope Paul, in his address to the pastors and preachers of Rome in 1965 made the following observation:

> The art of making preaching effective today should be one of the most important practical studies in modern pastoral training. We are brought to this conclusion by the example of speakers we hear daily on television, the cultural level of the people, the intolerance of contemporary man for every form of awkwardness, exaggeration, affected elegance, pseudoculture, or worldly substitutes for the sacred word. We are encouraged by present-day demands for plain, simple, essential, brief, and intelligible language. There remains the difficulty of expressing divine things in human language, of giving to the holy word that secret power which makes it compelling and salutary. The

religious life of our times must depend to a large extent on this human and mysterious efficacy of preaching.

This book is meant to help you in preaching according to the mind of Pope Paul, but it is only a help and not a short cut to a fully prepared homily. It cannot substitute for your own creative work after you have studied and prayed over the scriptural readings in the light of your people's current needs. The homilies are intended to give you one approach to the day's liturgy, and hopefully a spark or stimulus to your own thinking as you prepare your homily. At best the words in this book are nothing more than cold, black print on a page. Only you the preacher can make what is behind these words come alive as real spiritual communication.

The office of preaching is your gift from God by which you are to "utter his praises in the vast assembly" (Ps 22: 26) as you lead the people to know Jesus Christ in the breaking of the bread.

C. E. M.

First Sunday of Advent

A SECOND CHRISTMAS

As we begin Advent today the Church tells us that Christmas is coming. It looks like the Church is pretty late, however, with her announcement. All the stores have long ago put up their decorations and displays, and every now and then you can catch a Christmas carol on the radio. Some children are by now on the fourth or fifth revision of their list of presents they want from Santa Claus, and little boys and girls are already eagerly asking, "How many more days to go?" Anybody who doesn't know that Christmas is coming must have been living on another planet, and it seems about time that the Church has finally gotten around to telling us to get ready.

Another Christmas

And yet we can look pretty hard at today's scriptural readings without finding any idea about the birth of Jesus. The reason is that there are two Christmasses we have to think about. The first is the one we know so well, the coming of Jesus Christ into the world through his birth at Bethlehem. Jesus was born a man like us in all things but sin in order to teach us how to live both by his words and by his example. He won for us our freedom from sin and gave us the means to fulfill the purpose of human existence. Now he has left his human home, this earth, to go to his Father's home in heaven. But he will return. There will be a second Christmas. This second Christmas is the coming of Christ into the world at the end of time. Maybe we don't give that coming

BREAKING THE BREAD

enough thought, and so the Church wisely on this first Sunday of Advent calls our attention to this second coming.

A *"Christmas" List*

When Jesus does return he will want to know how we have followed his teachings and what use we have made of the means he has given us to make something of our lives. However, our expectation of the second Christmas should be a joyful and happy one, in much the same spirit as we await our celebration of Christmas day. Though Jesus is certainly no Santa Claus, he will come as a gift-giver, and we should have our list of desired presents ready for him, a list that may need a little revising. Of course we all want the gift of happiness, but perhaps in the past our list has been a trifle childish in what we have been asking for in prayer—things like financial success, health, the overcoming of loneliness and frustrations. All these things are worth asking for, but we must remember that they are like so many presents we get at Christmas which don't last very long. In comparison with what Jesus has to offer they are actually scarcely better than some inexpensive toy with which a child plays for a while but soon breaks or tires of. The gift that Jesus wants to give is eternal life—something impossible for us to imagine, for no ear has ever heard, no eye has ever seen the wonderful gift that God has for those who wait for him.

Stay Awake!

And wait we must with perseverance and patience. "Stay awake," Jesus says in the gospel. "Do not let him come suddenly and catch you asleep." You have seen little children who on Christmas eve want desperately to stay awake for the coming of Santa Claus but who just can't keep their eyes open, despite all their eagerness and impatience. We cannot afford to fall asleep because of weariness in our struggle to be faithful to the teaching of Christ. Nor must we grow impatient, thinking that Jesus will never come to right the wrongs of this world and to give us the present he has promised.

How Soon?

Maybe if we knew just when Jesus will come again, we could be more enthusiastic and zealous. "How many more days, or years, to go?" To that question Jesus refuses to give an answer. He simply says, "You do not know when the appointed time will come. Be constantly on watch!" Part of our faith and trust is to believe that Jesus will come at what is the best time in his divine plan. Our concern must be to keep watching, well prepared for his return. We have a pledge that, if we but cooperate, God will strengthen us to the end, so that we will be blameless on the day of Christ's coming.

Joyful Hope

We have the power to make the Second Christmas either joyful and happy, or fearful and terrifying. If we are loyal and persevering, we can be eager about the coming of Christ— eager, not anxious, for anxiety means a painful uneasiness of mind over an impending evil. Jesus does not will evil for us. He wants to give us a marvelous Christmas present, eternal life. The spirit that we should have—the spirit of the Second Christmas—is summed up in our prayer following the "Our Father": "In your mercy keep us free from sin and protect us from all anxiety as we wait in joyful hope for the coming of our Savior, Jesus Christ."

C. E.M.

Solemnity of the Immaculate Conception

FOLLOW THE LEADER

Over twenty years ago this day in a small town on an island in the Pacific the skies were aglow and there was ferocious activity. But it wasn't a celebration. The imperial war machine the morning before had gutted Pearl Harbor. Twenty-four hours later fires were still burning and men were being hauled out of partially submerged ships. The shock of war had touched American soil. These were to be days of sadness, waste, and destruction, but also times for unusual bravery. And the bravest heroes seem to have been the ones who thought they couldn't do much; but they started and others followed. Bravery seems almost contagious. Yet someone has to volunteer first.

World Crisis

Two thousand years ago the world faced a great crisis. A cosmic power was needed to straighten our life and make some sense of human suffering. A brave person was needed to begin the process, an instrument chosen by God and made fit by him through an immaculate conception, someone who could be both humble and effective. Courageously a young woman, so chosen and made fit by God, volunteered—a young woman who took credit for nothing, "the maidservant of the Lord," but who with God's grace could say, "Let it be done to me as you say."

Follow Her Lead

Someone has to be bold and go first to show the rest of us what is possible. Mary had to take the great leap of faith

Solemnity of the Immaculate Conception

and trust totally in God's will. The one to go first seems to have the hardest road. Mary had to care for a child and see the Son of God. Mary had to hear her son ridiculed as a madman and see the Messiah. She had to experience his death as a criminal and know her son to be a king. But she did it. So it's not so hard for us to follow the lead. Mary's faith strengthened the apostles and it should strengthen us.

We blame mother Eve for foolishly blazing the trail of listening to Satan, of having faith in pride and self-power. But as the early Church Fathers shouted, we praise mother Mary for making a path for the humble pilgrim, to have faith in Jesus Christ as our total answer, the real way of becoming "like God." We have been "predestined through Christ to be adopted sons," and we have been predestined through Mary to be believing pilgrims.

Ask Now

During this Mass, simply ask Mary to gently hold your hand, as only a mother can, and guide you through any shadows you may be experiencing. Think about the events in Christ's life and consider how Mary responded. Ask her son to share his Spirit with you as he did with his mother. And ask the Holy Spirit dwelling in Mary to fill each of us with the courage to believe Jesus is Lord, to be strong enough to live openly as dedicated Christians.

There may not be visible wars in your neighborhood demanding bravery, but the war of Satan, enflamed by man's pride, continues to saturate us. Go ahead: take up Christ and wave the banner of faith. Who knows, you may start a movement.

M. M. R.

Second Sunday of Advent

BEGINNING AND END

Today's gospel reading was the beginning of the holy gospel according to Mark. During this liturgical year we will be hearing more of Mark's gospel than of the other three as the mystery of Christ is unfolded Sunday after Sunday. Since you would expect the beginning of a gospel to center around the birth of Jesus, the verses we just heard seem to be a strange starting point. Mark takes up his narrative when Jesus was already a grown man, heralded by John the Baptist. Mark is not so much concerned with the fact that Jesus was born as he is with the reason why he was born and came into our world. His main purpose was to present Jesus as the savior, as the Man-God who came to lead man back to God.

Meaning

Mark's approach is of great value. It should make us stop and think. Certainly we treasure the beautiful stories of Christ's birth as found in Matthew and especially in Luke, but for some people Christmas seems to mean little more than a charming narrative which serves as a setting for a myriad of carols. No doubt this year we will again hear the plea, "Put Christ back into Christmas." And it is a plea which needs to be made. But that plea is not heeded merely by making sure our Christmas cards depict a nativity scene or even by placing a crib next to the tree. These things we should do, but they have meaning only if we do them with the reali-

Second Sunday of Advent

zation of why God the Father gave us the first Christmas gift, his own Son, and with faith in what Jesus came to accomplish.

The Baptist

In the beginning God made man in his own likeness, and set him over the whole world to serve him and to rule over all creatures. Our first parents had the ability to know God and to love him—to be his friends. But they lost God's friendship through sin, something that human beings have been doing ever since. As a result our world fell into turmoil, filled with confusion, hatred and greed, leading to death. And yet at no time did God give up on his creation or abandon the human race. Again and again God offered a renewal of friendship and through the prophets taught men to hope for salvation. Slowly and gradually people began to realize that one day God would send a personal savior to right the wrongs of the world and firmly re-establish a relationship of love and friendship between himself and the human race.

Mark began his presentation of Jesus with the story of John the Baptist, the last of the Old Testament prophets. In a sense John summed up in his preaching the message of all the other prophets. "Get ready," he said, "the savior is here, the one who is greater than I." As Mark developed his gospel he showed that Jesus Christ is the expected savior, not just another prophet, but God himself who became a man like us in all things but sin. Most importantly he emphasized that Jesus saved us through his death and resurrection. Jesus destroyed death and restored life as he bridged the gap separating mankind from God.

BREAKING THE BREAD

Past and Future

The beginning of Mark's gospel makes us think back to the past, to the beginning of our human history. Jesus came as a savior because of a long history of failure on the part of human beings. Jesus has beyond doubt given us the means of salvation, but anyone who has eyes to see can perceive that our world is still filled with confusion, hatred and greed leading to death. As a matter of fact, the coming of Jesus stands between two extremes of human history, its beginning and its end. It took long centuries of waiting for God to send Jesus into the world, and it is taking long centuries of waiting before the saving work of Jesus takes full effect.

New Heavens and New Earth

In today's second lesson St. Peter, like an Old Testament prophet, teaches us to hope for the complete salvation promised by God. He begs us not to be impatient or to think that God is delaying his work unnecessarily. God has a plan which he is carefully working out. St. Peter says, "What we await are new heavens and a new earth where, according to his promise, the justice of God will reside." John the Baptist preached repentance as a preparation for the first coming of Christ, and St. Peter preaches the same message as a preparation for the second coming of Christ. He says, "So beloved, while waiting for this, make every effort to be found without stain or defilement, and at peace in his sight."

This Christmas

In a short time we will once again commemorate the birth of Jesus, a coming which marked the turning point in human history. We should celebrate Christmas in the traditional way, with all its decorations and carols in a spirit

Second Sunday of Advent

of joy. But we should realize that the happiness of Christmas is only a shadow of what still awaits us in the second coming of Christ. We are a people of hope who yearn for the saving work of Jesus to take its full effect as we look for a new heaven and a new earth.

C. E. M.

Third Sunday of Advent

DO YOU RECOGNIZE HIM?

When a man has something important on his mind, something that is really bothering him, he finds it pretty hard to hold it back. If he is talking to you, he probably will bring up the subject before very long. When St. John composed his gospel, it took him only eleven verses to get to something that was bothering him. After proclaiming that the eternal Son of God came into our world, he made this melancholy statement: "To his own he came, yet his own did not accept him." And just a few verses later he quoted the words of the Baptist which we heard read only moments ago: "There is one among you whom you do not know." The failure of people to recognize and accept Christ was still on John's mind when he came to the conclusion of the gospel. Because he wanted to make sure that his listeners would not make the same mistake as others, he said: "These things have been recorded to help you believe that Jesus is the Messiah, the Son of God...."

Failure

John's gospel was not written down until the end of the first century. By that time its central message had been preached and proclaimed for about sixty years. Moreover, many passages from the Old Testament, such as the one we heard today as our first reading, had been read and understood by the Church in the light of a further and full revelation which brought the figure of Jesus Christ into a gradually sharper focus. For John the Apostle the truth of Jesus Christ

Third Sunday of Advent

was a clear, living reality. It must have been absolutely incredible to him as he neared the end of his life that many people still failed to recognize or to accept Jesus Christ.

Incredible

If John the Apostle were alive today, I wonder what he would think of people and their faith. Would he observe that all of his apostolic efforts had produced results in the twentieth century? Perhaps we can agree that he would find it incredible that in our modern world so many people still fail to recognize or accept Christ. But maybe we have arrived at the right answer while looking in the wrong direction. If we are thinking of all the irreligious people, the atheists, the pagans of our own times as a cause for John's disappointment, we are not focusing on the real problem. John would want to know whether we who profess to be Christians have really accepted Christ. Could it be that he would find it necessary to quote the words of the Baptist to us: "There is one among you whom you do not recognize."

Hidden

We believe that Jesus is the Messiah, the Son of God. We accept the reality of his presence in the Blessed Sacrament. But there should be more. Jesus is not only glorified in heaven and sacramentally present in the Eucharist. He is among us today. Do we recognize him? When Jesus walked this earth, his divinity was hidden beneath the veils of his humanity. Only faith could see through those veils to his true identity. Today Jesus is hidden beneath the humanity of the persons with whom we live. Only faith can see through that humanity to the person of Jesus Christ.

BREAKING THE BREAD

Christmas Spirit

We will soon renew our faith in Jesus through the celebration of Christmas. We will profess our belief that the little baby born of Mary in Bethlehem is the Messiah, the Son of God. Once again the "Christmas spirit" hopefully will fill us with the feeling of good will toward our fellow men as we write cards, give gifts, and greet others with a joyful "Merry Christmas." One of the nicest things about Christmas is the effort that everyone makes to be pleasant, agreeable, and helpful. No one wants to be another Scrooge at this time of the year. But the birth of Jesus is not just an historical event of the past which is commemorated each December. Jesus is born again and again in our fellow human beings. The Christmas spirit of love should not be confined to the last two weeks of this month. Rather it should endure all year. Why can't we keep that spirit in January and through all the other months? I don't think the basic reason for our failure is that we are bad or that we don't care about others or that we are selfish. I think the basic problem is that we don't have real faith that Jesus is living in others, that what we do, good or bad, to even the least of his brethren, we do, good or bad, to him.

Deep Faith

In the second lesson St. Paul urged us to never cease praying. That is more than good advice. It indicates an absolute necessity for having the deep faith required of us. Deep faith is a gift from God which he gives in answer to earnest, persevering prayer. It is a gift well worth praying for in this Mass and everyday because it can transform our lives. If we had the faith to recognize Jesus among us, we could have Christmas every day this coming year.

Third Sunday of Advent

St. Paul today also had a Christmas wish for us: that we may be found irreproachable at the coming of Jesus Christ. When Jesus comes again to judge us, he will have something on his mind and it will not take him long to get to the point. He will want to know, not only whether we have accepted him as the Messiah, but also whether we have recognized him as he truly lives in our fellow human beings.

C. E M.

Fourth Sunday of Advent

GOD'S CHRISTMAS PREPARATIONS

The time before Christmas is a time of preparation: writing last minute Christmas cards, purchasing a tree, and planning a menu. Most important of all is the selecting of gifts for relatives and friends. We spend the most thought, time, trouble, and expense on the gifts that will go to the persons whom we love the most.

God's Preparation

Of course we give gifts at Christmas only because God started the whole idea. The gifts that we give others should be a reminder of the great Gift God gave to us on the first Christmas. That first Christmas was a long time in coming. God in a sense spent much thought on his Gift. His plan was a mystery hidden for ages (second reading). God had the intention of giving us his Gift all along, even before he created the world, but when sin became a reality his Gift took on a new value and preciousness.

God put a lot of time and trouble into the preparation for his Gift. In fact the entire Old Testament is the story of his preparation. First God selected a man, Abraham, to be the father of his chosen people, the Hebrews. Abraham had a son Isaac, and Isaac had a son Jacob, who in turn had twelve sons, from whom came the twelve tribes of Israel. These people, in time of famine, went into Egypt where they enjoyed the protection of one of the twelve sons, Joseph. Following the death of Joseph, the Israelites became enslaved in Egypt until they were led by Moses to freedom in the Exodus. After wandering in the desert for forty years,

Fourth Sunday of Advent

the Israelites were established in the promised land where God made a further selection in preparation for his Gift. He decreed that the savior would come from among one of the twelve tribes, that of Juda. From among the members of that tribe, the Jews, he chose one family, that of David. The prophecy of Nathan, which we heard in the first reading, formed the basis for Jewish expectation of a Messiah. The promise that David's kingdom and throne would endure forever was brought to a focus through Mary in the event described in today's gospel. Mary was told that the child to be conceived in her womb by the Holy Spirit would be given the throne of David, his father. Nine months later the Messiah was born in Bethlehem, David's home town. Throughout the lengthy history of salvation in the Old Testament God was very patient and painstaking in his preparations. The Gift took a long time in coming, but all the waiting was worth it. God gave us a wonderful Gift. He loved us so much that he gave us his own Son.

The Wrappings

When some people give you a Christmas gift they go to great trouble to wrap it as elegantly as possible. Once in a while the wrappings are so extravagant that you are disappointed when you open the gift. God did just the opposite with his Gift. He wrapped his Gift in a plain, ordinary way, for Jesus did not come robed in the finery of regal elegance amid the splendid trappings of a royal court in a leading city of the world. He was born just as human as we are except for sin, of a humble Jewish girl in an out-of-the-way place within the little-known town of Bethlehem. One of the great appeals of Christmas is that the eternal Son of God in the simplest manner possible became flesh and made his dwelling among us.

BREAKING THE BREAD

Thanks and Praise

We are the ones who benefit by all the preparations God made. We are the ones who enjoy his precious Gift. Jesus has really been given to us. He has entered our history, our world, our lives. Though Jesus came at one point in history, and in one definite place, his coming has value and significance for all men of all times and places. Jesus means everything to us. It is no wonder that at Christmas we are joyful and happy. But besides being joyful and happy, we should be grateful to God for his Christmas gift to us. In the preface we will say, "Father, all-powerful and ever-living God, we do well always and everywhere to give you thanks...." When we reflect on the meaning of Christmas we know that we have a special motive for thanksgiving at this time of the year. In this Mass we should lift our minds and hearts and voices in gratitude to God who has been so generous with us.

And as we go about our final preparations for Christmas, we should let those preparations be a reminder to us of all the thought, time, and trouble that God put forth in preparing to send us our great Gift, his own son.

C. E. M.

Christmas Eve (Afternoon or evening Mass)

A CHANGE IS MADE

Tomorrow will be Christmas. We have looked forward to its coming for three weeks, but in just a few hours it will all be over for another year. But should we let Christmas just come and go? Should it not make a difference in our lives that will last beyond the one day of Christmas?

Christ Came to Change the World

When Christ was born twenty centuries ago he changed the whole course of history. With his birth time stopped in a sense, and men began to count time all over again. Christ, however, is not satisfied with a mere change in the reckoning of time. He wants to work a change in the life of each one of us.

How People Change Our Lives

Everyone knows what it means to have a person change his life. Take a young man, for example, in his early twenties. Before he gets married he may lead a rather carefree, happy-go-lucky existence. He has a pretty good job, but he is not too worried about it; he feels he can always get another one. He spends his money freely on the things he likes to do without much concern. But one day he gets married and everything changes because a new person has entered his life. Now he has to become responsible and reliable. He makes sure that he is on the job because he knows that someone is depending on him. He begins to follow a budget and tries to save as much as he can. In a way he may

BREAKING THE BREAD

feel that he has given up a little of his freedom, but he does not mind because he loves the person who has changed his life. In fact his new life brings him a much greater happiness than he ever knew as a carefree bachelor.

Somewhat the same is true of a woman once she becomes a mother. The new baby makes her life very different. She has to turn a lot of her attention to her child. She has to feed him, bathe him, care for him in every way. The helpless baby takes away a lot of his mother's freedom, but a good mother does not mind. In fact she is happy about it because she loves her baby.

Jesus Changed the Life of Mary and Joseph

Jesus certainly worked a change in the life of Mary, his Mother. Of course Jesus was a normal baby in the sense that he had all the needs of any other baby, and it was Mary who met these needs. But Jesus changed the life of Mary in a fuller sense. After all, who would Mary have been without Jesus? She would have been just another devout Jewish girl who would have grown up, raised a family, and died. But with Jesus Mary is the greatest saint in heaven, conceived without sin, and sharing with Jesus in his great work of the salvation of the world.

The gospel of today shows us how Jesus changed the life of Joseph. Joseph was a good man, a carpenter, in love with a girl called Mary. He was engaged to her and was looking forward to the day of his wedding. He probably expected to have an ordinary life like that of the other young men of his village. Then he discovered that Mary was going to have a child. Exactly what his thinking was is not absolutely clear from the gospel. Was he aware merely that Mary was pregnant, or did he already have an intimation that her state was the result of a special grace from God? It does not seem unlikely that he and Mary would have talked about the situation, and Mary would have told him the truth. In that case Joseph, being a humble man, felt that he had no place among these sacred circumstances and it was for this reason that he decided not to be so bold as to marry Mary, but to "divorce" her, or, as we would say, to break the engagement. He felt unworthy to share in this holy action of God. The word of the angel in the dream was a word of encouragement. The angel told him not to scruple to enter into this mystery of God. It was God's will that Jesus be a part of his life with Mary. And so it was that Jesus made of Joseph a great saint, worthy indeed to be patron of the universal Church.

Jesus Wants to Change our Lives

Jesus, through the grace of our Christmas celebration, wants to change our lives too. That is why Jesus came into the world with his revelation. The Vatican Council in its Constitution on Revelation says, "The obedience of faith must be given to God who reveals, an obedience by which man entrusts his whole self freely to God..." (5). Some people may feel that Jesus takes away our freedom. He requires that we follow his will, and tells us that if we love him we must keep his commandments. Sometimes we may even yearn to be "free." But Jesus has also told us that his yoke is sweet and his burden is light. Following the will of Jesus at times may feel like a burden, especially when we look around and see others doing apparently as they please without scruple. When all is said and done, however, it is only the love of Jesus that can make us completely happy. It is only the love of Jesus that can really make us free, free from the shackles of sin and the everlasting death that sin eventually brings to its slaves.

BREAKING THE BREAD

Jesus Invites Us

Actually the thing that ought to amaze us is that Jesus is even interested in us. We ought to be humble enough to wonder, like Joseph, that we can be so bold as to expect Jesus to become part of our lives. What right do we have to the grace and love of Jesus? Well might we hesitate if it were not for the fact that Jesus says, "Come to Me." In this Mass and in every Mass he invites us to receive him in Holy Communion. He wants to enter our lives to be that one Person above all others for whom we live, that one Person whom we love so much that we would never want to offend him or drive him from our lives. After the communion of this Mass we will pray, "Lord, grant us new life as we celebrate the birthday of your only-begotten Son." We should indeed pray for a new life, a life changed by the presence of Christ.

Conclusion

Yes, Christmas will come and go in just a few hours, but the effect of its grace can be a lasting one if we are only willing to let Jesus change our lives.

C. E. M.

THE BIRTH OF HOPE

The darkness of the night can suggest danger and hostility. It can arouse feelings of fear, uncertainty, and loneliness. It often is an especially difficult time for those who are sick, and yet the night can be a turning point for them. Those few who are keeping a quiet vigil at the bedside observe that the patient becomes restful; his temperature goes down; the crisis passes, and there is born in their hearts a new hope for recovery, health, and happiness.

A Turning Point

Some seven hundred years before Christ, Isaiah wrote in prophecy: "The people who walked in darkness have seen a great light; upon those who dwelt in the land of gloom a light has shone; you have brought them abundant joy and great rejoicing ... for a child is born ...." Christmas is the perfect fulfillment of those words, an event of great hope which took place in the dark stillness of night. It was the turning point for the whole human race sick almost to death with the illness of sin. The crisis passed with the birth of a child. Only a few observed the event: Mary, Joseph, and the shepherds, but they knew with joy beyond description that with the birth of Jesus there was born a new hope for recovery from sin, and a new hope for spiritual health and eternal happiness.

Sign of Hope

A newly born child is a natural sign of hope. His parents pray that he will grow and develop into someone important and famous, someone of value and worth. Many a father

BREAKING THE BREAD

has looked at his new son and said, "This kid can be President some day." We do not exactly know what the thoughts of expectation were in Mary's mind as she looked upon her son for the first time. We are not quite sure whether Mary even then had an image of how her son was to be of value and worth to his fellow human beings. As she looked on the smooth, soft infant's flesh which she had given him, did she know that she would see that flesh torn and lacerated in the crucifixion? Did she realize that the precious blood which was then giving a healthy hue to her baby's face would one day be drained from his body on the cross? These things we are not certain of, but when the day of sacrifice did come Mary understood that her son was giving himself for all of us, for our spiritual health and eternal happiness.

Where Is Peace?

Mary at Christmas looked to the future with hope. We now look to the past, not only upon the birth of Jesus, but also upon his death and resurrection, the means of our salvation. But we wonder where is the spiritual health, where is the happiness he came to bring? The world still seems sick with the illness of sin. There is poverty, hatred, and war, rather than peace on earth.

The Reason

The reason for all this *is* that salvation does not occur automatically. Each one of us *must* learn to live like Jesus, to share his love for God and for *our* fellow human beings. With his birth the turning point was *in*deed reached, the crisis was over. But much remains to be *do*ne before the world fully recovers. Each one of us individu*ally* must contribute to that recovery by the way in which we *live*. Our flesh will be torn and lacerated in the struggle against sin. Even our blood will be drained in the battle against hatred and war.

A New Birth

This Christmas, however, is a sign of joyful hope, because Christmas is meant to be a new birth for Jesus. Jesus gives us his flesh and blood in communion with the plea that we will give him our flesh and blood so that his goodness and love may continue in the world today. He wishes to be born again in us like a little baby, a baby who is a sign of hope.

C. E.M.

MISSION: IMPOSSIBLE

"Your mission, Ted and Teri, if you decide to accept this marriage agreement, is to form a holy family." Very truthfully, these words could be addressed to each couple during their wedding ceremony. And, if they were spoken by the presiding minister, almost everyone attending the wedding, including the bride and groom, would shout out, "Mission: Impossible." Our society has become more and more pessimistic about the possibility of forming a holy and happy family life. And, yet, this feast today in honor of the holy family of Jesus, Mary, and Joseph, presents us with just such a possibility.

Changing the Image

The liturgy today offers us a good image of family life. The wisdom of the Old Testament of the Bible is condensed in the first reading. It seems to me it would be advantageous to hear this read again slowly and meditatively. (*Read.*) You see, the image presented here is one of a positive and constructive view of the problems that usually confront our families today. Unfortunately, it has become more and more profitable, especially on television, to create laughs at the expense of the family image. If the laughter from the live audience is not loud enough, it is amplified with previously taped laughter. And so, a previously tarnished image is made further dull and uninspiring.

Feast of the Holy Family

Happiness Impossible?

Obviously, the recommendations in both the first and second readings seem to present an impossible task. And, yet, even if in your family you have not seen happiness work out, still you do know some families where it has. If you say that you don't know any, then one would have to reply that your experiences are not broad enough, or you are taking superficially imperfect situations as the norm, and not realizing the deeper happiness that is present, but seldom expressed to you. The fact that a priest is not married and thus does not experience directly the problems of achieving happiness in marriage must be admitted. However, his pastoral experience brings him into contact with a large variety of marriages. The sum total of these contacts is that happiness in family life is possible. Complete and absolute and total happiness? Obviously not. Such happiness is not possible in any human situation. But peace, contentment, enjoyment, good feelings, growing and developing personalities, positive thinking about the challenges of daily living together, all these and more are seen in the broad spectrum of family life that is the joy of any priest who gives his time and energy to the families under his care.

Improving the Image

Let's take a few minutes looking at some of these couples who have improved their image of family life. First, they realize the sacredness and permanence of the agreement that they made to be husband and wife, and hopefully, father and mother. For Catholics this sacredness is further enhanced by the sacrament of marriage received during the Mass. For some couples this realization was not present at the time of

BREAKING THE BREAD

the wedding, but gradually through prayer and study and consultation it came to be one of the main supports of a satisfying living together. The initial sacrament of their family relationship has been added to Sunday by Sunday by those couples who truly worship together at Mass and develop that feeling of closeness and unity which comes from receiving the bond of unity, holy communion. And the main bulwark of many couples against the forces that can tear them apart is that they honestly and openly listen to each other. Consequently there is not the effort on the part of one member to the marriage to make over the other in the image which he or she had that the other should be. When the lines of communication are always open, or if blocked temporarily, then opened again as soon as possible, most of the problems that interfere with the happiness of the family can be resolved. Surely, there are many problems that need outside help, but, if the couple are really talking to each other, then they will mutually realize this need and agree to seek such help. God help those who are not willing to be truly honest with one another! Many other good ways to happiness are seen in so many families. But let these few examples suffice for now.

Mission: Possible

The television show begins with what looks like an impossible situation. But once the team put their heads together, we know they will turn "Mission: Impossible" into "Mission: Possible." Why not look at happiness in marriage in that way? Then, the recommendations of St. Paul in the second reading today will not look like so much pious froth. No, the image of family life as given us by the holy family is a possible image for all those who truly wish it. Let us pray for all our families in this Mass, the beautiful Eucharist of peace, and harmony, and love, and happiness.

O. J. M.

Solemnity of Mary, the Mother of God
New Year's Day

RENEWAL

"May God bless us in his mercy." This is one of the nicest responsories we have during the entire year. And it is very appropriate for the beginning of a new year. There are many blessings we all need—in the whole world, in our nation, in our cities and towns, in our families and homes, and in our own individual lives. So, may God bless each of us through this new year.

Mary and Renewal

The blessings in the first reading when spoken by God to Moses were in relation to the renewal of the Hebrew people after their freedom from Egyptian slavery. Actually the entire history of these chosen people looked toward a freedom which would involve the entire human race. Even though these people thought of freedom only in relation to themselves, nevertheless God had in mind the renewal of all mankind in love and freedom—freedom once again to love God and all men for the sake of God. This universal freedom, this renewal, was realized in the coming of Christ, born of a woman. St. Paul stated, "When the designated time had come, God sent forth his Son born of a woman . . . so that we might receive our status as adopted sons."

The fathers of the Vatican Council re-affirmed the place of Mary, this woman, in God's plan of renewal, "truly the mother of God and mother of the redeemer." They pointed out that "in subordination to Christ and along with him, by the grace of almighty God she served the mystery of redemption" (Constitution on the Church, 56).

BREAKING THE BREAD

Our Mother

Mary responded to God's plan of redemption more completely than any other human person. Her example should give encouragement to us in our efforts to cooperate with God in the renewal of ourselves. Following Mary as a model, we should see New Year's resolutions as an expression of our own individual effort with God's grace to make the work of redemption effective here and now. Take anger, for example, anger which does real harm to the person who is angry and through him to others, such as the brutal beating of another, either of a young child by an irate parent, or of an old man by irresponsible youths. Some people say this kind of thing, though deplorable, is inevitable. God's plan of renewal says that gradually the peace of Christ and his meekness will envelope those persons afflicted with the sin of anger. And so with every other sin.

What we may not realize is that we do need the influence and help of a mother to become the better persons we should be through the grace of God. Again the fathers of the Vatican Council remind us of the role of Mary: "In an utterly singular way she cooperated by her obedience, faith, hope, and burning charity in the Savior's work of restoring supernatural life to souls. For this reason she is a mother to us in the order of grace .... By her maternal charity Mary cares for the brethren of her Son who still journey on earth surrounded by dangers and difficulties, until they are led to their happy fatherland" (*Ibid.*, 61f.).

Devotion

Certainly devotion is in place to anyone so intimately connected with God's renewal. One important form of devotion is imitation. In our devotion let us imitate Mary's great love for all of God's children. She was willing to become the spiritual mother of every human being, regardless of race, color, nationality, political beliefs, religious creed, looks, health, wealth, poverty, success, failure, appeal, drabness—I need not go on with the litany. Why do we make such distinctions when Mary never did? Mary loved everyone enough to bring Christ into the world for them. Why do we hold back in showing the love of Christ to the world?

On this first day of the new year when we celebrate the Solemnity of Mary, the Mother of God, an excellent resolution would be to imitate Mary in her love. Working toward fulfilling that resolution with God's grace will be working toward the renewal God has in mind for the entire world.

O. J. M.

Solemnity of the Epiphany

EQUALITY OF MAN BEFORE HIS CREATOR

In an unpretentious cemetery in Lancaster, Pennsylvania, you can see the grave of Thaddeus Stevens. Hardly any congressman worked harder for "equality of man before his Creator." He died in 1868, attended by two black nuns. His epitaph, composed by himself, can be read on his tombstone:

> I repose in this quiet and secluded spot,
> Not for any natural preference for solitude
> But, finding other Cemeteries limited as to Race
> by Charter Rules,
> I have chosen this that I might illustrate
> in my death
> The Principles which I advocated through a
> long life:
> Equality of Man before His Creator.
> (See *Reader's Digest,* July 1971, page 174)

Equality of Man before His Creator. This is one of the truths that the liturgy of the Epiphany is concerned with. It is a truth that concerns us today.

Equality in the Early Church

Christians in the early Church were confronted with the problem of exclusiveness. Like us they had been taught they were a chosen race, a royal priesthood, a special people, a people through whom salvation was to come. The early Christians inherited this idea from the Hebrew religion from which most of the first converts came. Were not the Hebrew

Solemnity of the Epiphany

people the chosen ones from whom would come the Savior of the world? Were they not the descendants of Abraham to whom the promise of redemption was given, and passed on through Isaac and Jacob and the twelve tribes that sprang from him? And did not Christ when he redeemed mankind transfer God the Father's choice from the Hebrew people to the new people of the new covenant, the followers of Christ? So it was natural for some of them to think of themselves as better than those who did not belong to their ranks. It was easy for them to forget that their faith was a gift from God and something they had not merited. Equality of all men before the Creator was admissible as a theory, but in practice there was a tendency among some Christians toward smugness and an attitude that their salvation was automatically assured, no matter how they led their lives. In theory we too readily admit, especially since the Second Vatican Council, the equality of all men before God, but in practice we can have a tendency toward exclusiveness and a complacent attitude of automatic salvation. Let us see how today's liturgy attempts to set straight our thinking in this matter.

Jerusalem, the Center

According to the first reading, Isaiah sees Jerusalem as the center of God's mercy. At last the time is coming when the glory of the Lord will shine upon this chosen city. Yes, Jerusalem is the chosen city of redemption, but the resulting salvation is not the exclusive right of the citizens of the city. For, "your sons come from afar ... all from Sheba shall come." And so our response to this word of God was: "Lord, every nation on earth will adore you." The universality of God's mercy is further illuminated by these words pronounced to us by the lector: "For he will rescue the poor man when he cries out, and the afflicted when he has no one to help him. He shall have pity for the lowly and the poor; the lives of the poor he shall save." Yes, it is true: "Lord, every nation on earth will adore you." This figure of speech is not entirely true, even in our own times, for many peoples still do not honor God. But the statement does emphasize the possibility of every single person ever to inhabit the earth being a subject of God's saving goodness.

Gentiles, Co-Heirs

In the second reading St. Paul speaks very bluntly. "In Christ Jesus the Gentiles (everyone who is a non-Jew) are now co-heirs with the Jews, members of the same body and sharers of the promise through the preaching of the gospel." That there is no exclusiveness in God's kingdom is so frequently mentioned by St. Paul as to become a commonplace. Even though he was a Jew himself, he had no difficulty in admitting the equality of man before his Creator. It is because God loves us that we, too, have equality before him. For our part we should recognize this equality in all other persons and strive therefore to give them what is rightfully their due. Even though St. Paul is speaking mainly in a religious sense of equality, nevertheless, the implications of this equality are found in every aspect of life. On the city, state and national scales equality in educational and employment opportunities are directed by the respective agencies. So are also housing, recreational facilities, medical care, transportation. When these agencies do not represent us as they should, or fail through ignorance or malice to offer reasonable equality, then we as citizens must demand an accounting of such agencies. But within the ambit of our own personal lives, such as the family and the neighborhood, we must exercise personal responsibility to see that we do not infringe on the equal rights of others. In fact, we should positively sup-

Solemnity of the Epiphany

port these rights in every way we possibly can. This is the lesson of equality of all men before their Creator that the liturgy teaches us today.

Matthew's View

The story of the Wise Men in today's gospel is part of St. Matthew's way of teaching the early Christians the universality of God's salvation plan. God does not despise poor Jewish shepherds, or the rich men from the east. How many and what other people came to see the infant, we do not know. But we can be sure that they were all graciously received. It is an interesting tradition that we retain the shepherds in the Christmas crib, even after the time of their visit is passed, and while we introduce the Magi into the scene. There is something in this that admits our equality before God.

Our Weekly Visit

Each week we come before the crib of the Mass, when once again the miracle of God dwelling with us is repeated, not in the form of an infant, but under the species of bread and wine. Like the Magi, we, too, come offering our gifts. Representatives of this congregation will carry to the altar the water, wine, and bread, as we prepare to offer ourselves with Christ to the Father. Let this offering of ourselves not be marred by feelings of prejudice, bigotry or discrimination. Rather let us be joyful that before God, our Creator, we stand as equals, redeemed in the precious Blood of Jesus Christ.

O. J. M.

THE BAPTISM OF OUR LORD
(Sunday following Jan. 6th)

Suggested use: **Penitential Rite C**

> You humbled yourself in the waters of the Jordan, Lord have mercy.
>
> You humbled yourself in submission to your Father's will, Christ have mercy.
>
> You humbled yourself in death on the cross, Lord have mercy.

BAPTISM AND HUMILITY

The human race from the beginning offended God by sin and continues to do so, and therefore is in need of redemption. Regardless of his own personal condition of sinlessness, Jesus knew that the Messiah, the Redeemer, had to take upon himself the sinful condition of mankind. And so the first act of his public life was an act of humility, going down into the Jordan river to be baptized by John. From this first act every other action was directed toward the completion of redeeming mankind. Christ's death on the cross, made present under the signs of bread and wine in this very Mass, was the culmination of a life of extraordinary humility.

No Human Respect

Jesus came for the sake of sinners. Although Jesus knew that his reputation would be stained, he did not hesitate to be friendly with the woman taken in adultery, to allow Mary Magdalene to approach him and to wash and kiss his feet, to go into the house of Zacchaeus and eat with him, to enter the home of the Roman centurion, to sit at the well of Jacob and bring the news of salvation to a foreign woman of ill repute. And sure enough, Jesus' reputation was tarnished, for the accusation was finally made, "He is a friend of sinners and publicans, and eats and drinks with them."

Beloved, Yet Humble

But the seal of approval was put upon Christ by God his Father, and that is all that really counted. When Jesus came up from the waters of the Jordan, his Father declared: "You are my beloved Son. On you my favor rests." When we came from the water of our baptism, God said of us: "You are my beloved son. On you my favor rests." And that is what really counts—not what others may think of us or even what we may think of ourselves. But as Jesus did not take the words of his Father as an excuse to refuse to associate with sinful mankind, so we, even though beloved by the Father, must not think that we are too good for any fellow human being. We must not fall into the trap of self-righteousness, thinking that we are better than others. St. Peter's words in the second reading set us on the right track: "I begin to see how true it is that God shows no partiality. Rather, the man of any nation who fears God and acts uprightly is acceptable to him. This is the message he has sent to the sons of Israel, 'the good news of peace' proclaimed through Jesus Christ who is Lord of all."

Opinion of Others

If we are to follow the humility of Christ, then one thing we must do. In the decisions we make we must be careful lest the opinions of others sway us from the truth or from that which we know we must do. Jesus could have saved himself from death on the cross—yes, but only at the expense of compromising the truth and going back on what he knew was his calling in life, that of redeeming mankind. Many of the

BREAKING THE BREAD

decisions we make can be good or bad. A lot depends on what is behind them. The virtue of humility demands that we know the "why" of our decisions, which means that we face up honestly to our motives. Our concern for what others think of us is not necessarily evil, but if it makes us do things we know are wrong, then its influence is bad. We should recognize that we are God's children and that he loves us, but we must never use that truth as an excuse for turning our backs on those who are labeled as sinners or those whom we may find to be displeasing to us.

The Mass

Yes, Christ's death on the cross, made present for us here in the Mass, was the culmination of a life of extraordinary humility. As we now enter upon the eucharistic sacrifice, we should do so with the faith that we are indeed beloved by God, but we must also recognize that our offering will be pleasing only if we share in the humility of Christ.

O. J. M.

Second Sunday of the Year

CHRIST AND HIS PEOPLE

Two weeks ago we celebrated the epiphany of our Lord, his manifestation to the Magi. A star pointed out the infant Jesus as the savior of the world. Today we celebrate a manifestation of the adult Jesus as savior of the world. This time he is pointed out, not by a star, but by the prophet, John the Baptist. As Jesus walked by, John said to two of his own disciples, "Look! There is the Lamb of God!"

The Lamb in Egypt

The title, "Lamb of God," seems at first a strange designation for John to use. Actually the phrase is rich in biblical connotation. It recalls the exodus of the Israelites from slavery in Egypt. When God sent his avenging angel to kill all the first-born of the Egyptians, the Israelites sprinkled the blood of a sacrificial lamb on their doorposts. The angel seeing the blood passed over the homes of the Israelites. They were saved by the blood of the lamb. Then the Israelites were led by Moses through the waters of the Red Sea out of the slavery of Egypt and to freedom. The exodus formed the Israelites into the people of God. It was the great saving event of the Old Testament, comparable to the death and resurrection of Jesus in the New Testament.

The Lamb of God

We have no idea of how fully John the Baptist understood the phrase, Lamb of God, but when John the Evangelist wrote his gospel in the light of full revelation he saw the implications of that title. We have been saved from the slavery of sin through the blood of Jesus Christ shed on the cross, and we have become members of his Church, the new people of God, by passing through the waters of baptism. Though our vocation has been less dramatic, we have been called as definitely as was Samuel who heard God speak his name in the night (first lesson). God spoke our name through the priest who baptized us. We have been chosen just as surely as were those men who left the Baptist to become apostles of Christ. With Andrew we can say, "We have found the Messiah."

Effect

The effect of our Christian call is almost staggering. To begin with Jesus Christ is not some figure of ancient history lost within the pages of the New Testament. Jesus lives today! And we are really much more than his followers. We have become part of him, part of his mystical body. Yes, Jesus lives today—in heaven, in the eucharist, and in us!

I believe that most Catholics are familiar with the teaching of Jesus that whatever we do to his brethren, good or bad, we do to him, good or bad. We must guard against watering down that doctrine. Jesus did not say that what is done to others he *considers* as being done to himself, as, for example, a parent might consider a favor or an insult done to his child as done to himself. Because Jesus really lives in his followers, what is done to them is done to Jesus. We must also recognize that the converse is equally true. Jesus wants to act in and through us. We take him with us wherever we go, for good or bad. He is present within us in everything we do, good or bad. Listen again to these emphatic words of St. Paul in today's second lesson: "Do you not see that your bodies are members of Christ? Whoever is joined to the Lord becomes one spirit with him."

Second Sunday of the Year

Motive

For St. Paul the presence of Jesus within a Christian was the motive for avoiding sin, as well as for doing good. Regarding sexual sins Paul made a statement which is indeed very bold, so bold that if he had not made it, I doubt that any non-inspired writer would have done so. He wrote: "Would you have me take Christ's members and make them members of a prostitute? God forbid! Can you not see that the man who is joined to a prostitute becomes one body with her? Scripture says, 'The two shall become one flesh.'"* This doctrine carries over into other sins. When we are petty and mean, when we spread slander or detraction, when we are hateful and envious, Jesus is with us and we drag him through the filth of our sins. It is a chilling thought, but it is true.

A very practical approach is to ask ourselves, "Would Jesus do what I am about to do, or say what I am about to say, or even think what I am now tempted to think?" We should not make Jesus a part of something we know he would never do, or say, or think himself. More positively we should ask ourselves, "What would Jesus do in this situation?" The answer should help us decide what our conduct should be.

A New Epiphany

Jesus will come to us again today in holy communion. Through the eucharist he wants to transform us into himself so that we may become more and more a part of the mystical body. We must cooperate by promising him that we will

---

* The quotation is from the second half of the fifteenth and from the sixteenth verse of today's second lesson. For some unknown reason the compilers of the lectionary decided to omit these words from the pericope. Their decision was unfortunate, to say the least.

BREAKING THE BREAD

try to act only as we know he would act so that his presence in this world may continue through us. When Jesus was an infant, the star pointed him out to the Magi. When Jesus was an adult, the Baptist pointed him out to the apostles. Now we can point to heaven or to the eucharist and say to others, "There is Jesus." But Jesus wants more. He wants us to be able to point to ourselves and say, "Here is Jesus—living and acting within me."

C. E. M.

Third Sunday of the Year
Suggested Use: Penitential Rite A

FAITH AND REPENTANCE

When we hear of Jonah in the Bible, most of us think of the incident in which he was swallowed by the great fish. Actually that story was but a prelude to today's first lesson. God wanted Jonah to preach to the pagan city of Nineveh, but Jonah felt that only Jews should hear the word of God, and so he tried to run away. In a storm at sea, brought on by God's anger, he was cast into the water only to be swallowed by the fish and then vomited on the shore. He received a second command from God, to preach to the pagans of Nineveh. That time he obeyed, and much to his surprise the people heeded the word of God and repented.

Jesus Preaches

So-called fire and brimstone sermons of the type preached by Jonah are no longer popular. Nor would such a sermon be appropriate for you since your very presence at Mass is a sign of your good will. You would probably be shocked and dismayed to hear me stand in the pulpit and shout out like a modern day Jonah: "Repent! The end is coming." And yet in today's gospel we hear Jesus himself proclaim: "This is the time of fulfillment. The reign of God is at hand! Reform your lives and believe in the good news."

Shortly after he appeared in Galilee preaching the need for repentance and faith, Jesus called Andrew and Peter and James and John away from their work as fishermen to make them fishers of men. That same call Jesus continues to extend to bishops and priests down through the centuries. The reason is that his message of faith and repentance is

BREAKING THE BREAD

a message for people of all times and all places. And so it is that the Vatican Council in its Constitution on the Liturgy stated: "The Church announces the good tidings of salvation to those who do not believe, so that all men may know the true God and Jesus Christ whom he has sent, and may be converted from their ways, doing penance" (9). Then, perhaps to your surprise, the Council said in the same document: "To believers also the Church must ever preach faith and penance" (*ibid*).

Need for Repentance

Yes, even to believers the Church must constantly preach faith and penance. The penance referred to is perhaps better termed "repentance." Repentance means a turning away from sin and a turning toward God, a true change of heart necessary for all of us. To begin with, we are all really converts to the faith. No one can be born a Catholic in the way which we can be born an American citizen. Even if we were baptized as infants, at some time we must make for ourselves a profession of faith and a decision to follow Christ. Perhaps you are one of those persons who has taken your religion for granted—you are a Catholic simply because that is the way you were brought up. Today Jesus says to you: "Reform your life and believe in the good news!" Now is the time to realize that Jesus is the only way to salvation, and that your whole life must be based on his teachings. Money cannot save you, nor friends, nor society, nor the state. Only Jesus can make your life a success.

Special Grace

A middle-aged man had been what is sometimes called a "Sunday" Catholic. His religion had meant little more than going to Mass once a week. Then he was informed that his wife was to undergo surgery because of cancer. The doctors promised no hope. Suddenly he felt all alone and helpless. On the morning of the operation he decided to go to Mass to pray for his wife. By sheer coincidence it was Ash Wednesday. He followed the crowd of people toward the altar to receive the ashes. As they were placed on his forehead he heard the priest say, "Remember, man, that you are dust and unto dust you shall return." In that very instant he was struck with the shortness of life and he realized that not only was his wife close to death but that he himself was inevitably going to die at a time he knew not. That night his wife was dead. Through his grief he could see that even the longest life is short, and that time is precious.

Now Is the Time

Yes, time is precious. It is so precious that God gives it to us only moment by moment, and he never gives us a single moment without taking the previous one away. If we have squandered or abused a moment of time, we can do nothing to change it. All that is left is for us to work harder in the future. The earliest Christians believed that the entire world as we know it would soon pass away in the second coming of Christ. That was one of their motives for taking their religion seriously. As a matter of fact we simply do not know when Christ will come again, but we do know the world will end in effect for each one of us the day we die. Now is the time to repent, to have a change of heart, to "re-form" our lives in accord with the teachings of Christ. At the beginning of each Mass we are invited to examine our consciences, to consider not only the sins we commit but also the good we fail to do. Every one of us can stand some soul searching to determine what is holding us back from following Jesus

BREAKING THE BREAD

completely. This is a very personal, individual matter. The answer will be different for each one. But an answer we must find if we are to heed the words of Jesus: "Reform your lives and believe in the good news."

C. E M.

Fourth Sunday of the Year

JESUS, LORD AND SAVIOR

It is very difficult for us to appreciate the full impact of the simple gospel narrative we have just heard. We have become accustomed to hearing stories of how Jesus preached to the people and worked miracles for them, but those who first encountered Jesus many centuries ago were astounded by him. There was no doubt in their minds that Jesus was different from the prophets and doctors of the law. It was not until after the resurrection, however, that it became clear how different Jesus was from those who had communicated God's will to the people.

The Prophets

The chosen people all through their history had sought communication from God. In his concern for them God raised up prophets like Moses and Isaiah and Jeremiah. A prophet was a spokesman, a "mouthpiece," for God, one who spoke on his behalf to the people. Frequently a prophet prefaced his words with the phrase, "Thus says the Lord God." This phrase indicated that the prophet was speaking not on his own authority, but solely on God's authority, according as God has manifested his will to him. God promised through Moses that one day he would send a great prophet, as we heard in the first reading. After the resurrection, the Church understood that this promise was eminently fulfilled in Jesus Christ (cf. Ac 3:22ff and 7:37ff). Actually Jesus was much more than a prophet. He spoke on his own authority. Not once did he preface his remarks with the usual phrase, "Thus says the Lord God." Rather he proclaimed, "*I say to you....*" It was a bold departure, one which did not go unnoticed.

The Scribes

The people also observed that Jesus taught differently from the scribes, the official experts in written law and oral tradition. The scribes instructed the people by quoting the famous teachers of the past, somewhat in the manner in which a contemporary lawyer refers to previous court decisions. But Jesus spoke on his own and never made appeals to the testimony of others. His way of teaching was so different that he held the people spellbound.

Miracles

If Jesus held the people spellbound with the authority of his words, he amazed them with the power of his deeds. Jesus freed possessed persons from the presence of evil spirits. He did so simply, sometimes with a single word. These miracles signified in action what he preached in words. He proclaimed that in himself the kingdom of God had come, a divine kingdom that would be victorious over the forces of evil. When the people saw what Jesus did, they exclaimed, "He gives orders to unclean spirits and they obey him!"

Need

Jesus showed by words and deeds that he was Lord and Savior. Do we need Jesus today in the battles of life? We may think that we are more sophisticated than the people of Jesus' time. What they attributed to the presence of unclean spirits, we would perhaps classify as epilepsy or some form of psychosis, such as schizophrenia. And yet we would be unfair to today's gospel if we were to pretend that it does

Fourth Sunday of the Year

not describe the real exorcism of real devils.* After all, modern psychiatry does not satisfactorily indicate the origin of all disturbances, especially those particular cases in which there are no organic causes. We would be naïve indeed if we were to think that a psychiatric description explains away the power of the devil in all instances. We need modern psychiatry, but we must not be so gullible or fatuous as to think that it alone, or any other human force, can be the savior of the world. We need both the teaching and the power of Jesus.

Evil

Within us all lurks a potential for evil, and the bible indicates that there are intelligent, powerful forces in the world, known as Satan or devils, ready to exploit that potential. Such teaching is in accord with reality. Look, for example, at Nazism and all its horrors: millions of people exterminated. How could any human person be so evil as to perpetrate such crimes? Adolf Hitler was probably insane, but maybe part of the cause of his insanity was the power of Satan. Communism began with a certain sincerity and good intention in the face of human need, but how did it become an enslaving monster today?

The devil puts ideas into people's heads under the guise of good. Look at the attack on the sacredness of human life in the movements for abortion, euthanasia, and compulsory sterilization, often by people who seem convinced that the movements are for the welfare of the human race. Or consider the blows dealt to human dignity under the banner of freedom in the sexual revolution: premarital sex, wife swapping, the disintegration of marriage and the family. Think of all the excuses we manufacture for our failure to treat all

* Cf. *The Four Gospels* by Bruce Vawter, C.M., p. 101.

BREAKING THE BREAD

men as brothers. Human perversity alone does not sufficiently explain such phenomena. Nor can our inability to end war be attributed solely to political ineptness or economic greed.

Jesus the Savior

Human intelligence and natural resources have come under the saving power of Jesus Christ. That is why we can and should use them for the good of the human race, but if we think that we can rely on human or earthly means alone we will find that we are pitted against a foe too powerful for us to overcome. Our faith, in the light of the resurrection of Jesus from the dead, tells us that he is Lord and Savior. That is why his words had such authority and his deeds such power. Those words and deeds are still a living reality among us, for Jesus is not dead. He is alive and waiting for us to turn to him with confidence as our Lord and Savior.

G. E M.

Fifth Sunday of the Year

HAPPILY FOREVER AFTER

A certain man of more than comfortable means was highly respected in his community. He had acquired his considerable wealth quite honestly, and he enjoyed the reputation of being a person of integrity and deep religious convictions. He doted on his seven sons and three daughters, though he sometimes worried about spoiling them with his generosity. In the eyes of his friends and neighbors, as we say, he had it made. Then suddenly everything went wrong. His business failed and he was left a pauper. During a party at his oldest son's house, the roof collapsed in a violent windstorm, killing all ten of his children. He himself was stricken with a strange disease, which his doctors could not diagnose or cure. And his wife was on the verge of leaving him.

Perennial Problem

This account was not found in a recent newspaper or magazine, though it could have been. It is the story of Job, from a book of the bible written about four hundred years before Christ.° That book tackles the perennial problem of why good people must suffer instead of being rewarded in this life by the God they faithfully serve.°° It is a problem

---

° Modern scholars differ widely in their dating of the Book of Job, placing it anywhere between 600 and 300 B.C., but at a time when people expected reward or punishment only in this life.

°° In the famous dialogue section Job and his friends never use the proper name of Israel's God, Yahweh (except for 12:9, probably a copyist's addition). One theory is that the author apparently wished to say that Job was not necessarily an Israelite, that the problem of the suffering just man is common to all humanity.

we face every day—not that we believe we are as virtuous as Job, but we do get to wondering why some people who seem to care nothing at all about God and religion apparently do so well in life while we must struggle with many forms of human suffering. Job wondered that too. His "friends" tried to convince him that he had to be guilty of some heinous sin that had brought on God's punishments. Job examined his conscience but could not honestly admit to any such sin. And yet his suffering continued to the point that he cried out, as we heard in the first reading, "I shall not see happiness again." Job pulled himself together and remained patient with God. In a sense he wanted to give God a chance. He was rewarded with a profound insight. Through God's grace he suddenly realized that no mere human being, with his inadequate notions of good and evil, reward and punishment, can possibly probe the depths of God's wisdom and justice in the handling of human affairs. A man is presumptuous indeed to criticize God's guidance of life. In the end Job received from God twice as much as he had possessed before, and he "lived happily ever after."

Jesus and Suffering

Jesus too was concerned with the problem of human suffering in all its forms. We saw him in today's gospel curing people who were afflicted in various ways, ranging from the simple fever of Peter's mother-in-law to diabolical possession. When he rose early the next morning he sought a quiet place to pray. During his prayer he possibly spoke with his Father about human suffering, for the misery of the people must have still occupied his mind. Soon, however, his prayer was interrupted by Peter and his companions who informed him that everybody was looking for him. We can only surmise that the people wanted more favors from him. Though Jesus made no comment, he seemed to rise from prayer with a

Fifth Sunday of the Year

renewed sense of purpose. He said: "Let us move on to the neighboring villages so that I may proclaim the good news there also. That is what I have come to do."

At first glance it appears that Jesus ignored the continued pleas of the people for help. If more cures were needed where he already was, why did he decide to move on? The reason is that he had not come to free people from all suffering in this life. He had come to preach that God's love is present and active in this world in the midst of even the worst adversity, that there is hope for eternal salvation and lasting happiness, and that somehow in God's plan suffering obediently accepted leads to that salvation and happiness. He used his power to cure in order to confirm his message and to give a hint, a kind of preview, of the perfect healing of human ills that would come only in heaven. He did not use his power to prevent his own suffering and death. Rather he freely embraced the cross because he knew the value of human suffering accepted in loving obedience to God. In the Mass we joyfully celebrate the sacrifice of the cross because of the glory to which it led Jesus and will one day hopefully lead us too.

New Dimension

With Jesus the answer to human suffering—an answer sought by Job, by ourselves, by everyone—takes on a new dimension. With Job we must still realize that we cannot begin to understand the wisdom and justice of God and that we are in no position to criticize God's guidance of the universe, but in the preaching and actions of Jesus we can see suffering in a new light. Suffering is not to be endured in some stoic fashion because we can do nothing about it or because we dare not revolt against God or because if we wait long enough we will have relief in this life as did Job, who lived happily ever after—until his death. The ultimate value

BREAKING THE BREAD

of human suffering is to be found only after death, or better, through death. If we suffer and die in union with Jesus, we will also rise with him to a new life wherein we will indeed live happily *for*ever after.

Faith

It is only natural for us to look to God for help in all the setbacks and problems of human existence. But if relief does not come, we must not call into question either God's wisdom or his justice or his love. In faith we must look to Jesus on the cross, the cross which led to the glory of resurrection, to see why we should accept suffering from God in loving obedience.

C. E M.

Sixth Sunday of the Year
Suggested Use: Penitential Rite A;
Preface for Sundays of the Year I

A PEOPLE SET APART

People these days probably look upon cancer as the most frightening of human afflictions. Among the contemporaries of our Lord, leprosy held the first place. Undoubtedly people at that time also died of cancer, but no one really understood it as a cause of death since it was internal and therefore invisible. Leprosy, though lacking the devastating effects of cancer, was external and loathsome to look upon. Because the disease was considered to be highly contagious, the leper was forced to live in isolation, away from his family and friends. More distressing for a devout Jew, however, was the fact that he was considered levitically unclean and as such unfit to share in the public worship of God. When St. Paul wrote to the Corinthians, as we read in the second lesson, "Whatever you do, you should do all for the glory of God," he was extending to his Christian converts the ideal of the chosen people. The Jews were a royal priesthood, a holy nation, a people set apart for the authentic worship of the one true God. The leper was cut off from this worshipping community.

The Cure

The leper in today's gospel revealed how desperate he had become by entering a town in order to seek out Jesus. Jesus was moved to pity, rather than horror, at the sight of the man and cured him. It is worth noticing that the gospel says that Jesus *touched* the man, something all others would have been afraid to do, not only because they feared contagion but because touching a leper rendered one also levitically unclean. Jesus manifested that he was compassionate, but more importantly he showed that, as the source of all spiritual cleanness, he himself could not be made unclean.

Jesus then sent the man to the Jewish priest, whose function was not that of a physician but a judge and interpreter of the Law. It was the prerogative of the priest to decide whether the man was now fit to undergo the purification rites which would join him once more to the worshipping community.

Penitential Rite

As we will acknowledge in today's preface, we are the new chosen race, a royal priesthood, a holy nation, a people set apart. Back in 1947 Pope Pius XII wrote, "All the faithful should be aware that to participate in the Eucharistic Sacrifice is their chief duty and supreme dignity." * In order to fulfill this chief duty with supreme dignity we too should be clean. There is, however, no levitical law in the Catholic Church; nothing external can make us unfit to worship God. Only sin, like an invisible cancer, can make us unworthy to celebrate the Eucharist in the company of the worshipping community. Our first cleansing was at baptism. Confession is a sacramental cleansing, necessary in the case of serious sin. The penitential rite at the beginning of Mass is intended to make us realize that we must be sorry for all sins, even little ones. We confess first to God because every sin offends him directly. We also confess to one another, to our spiritual brothers and sisters, because sin hurts others and lessens our bond of oneness with all of God's people. If we are sincere in our sorrow, we are touched by the forgiving hand of Jesus, the source of all cleanness.

This penitential rite has a positive purpose. Once we have asked forgiveness, we should then with a sense of freedom

* *Mediator Dei*, 80.

Sixth Sunday of the Year

from the disease of sin enter wholeheartedly into the celebration of Mass. To complete the quotation from Pope Pius XII, "All the faithful should be aware that to participate in the Eucharistic Sacrifice is their chief duty and supreme dignity, *and that not in an inert and negligent fashion, giving way to distractions and daydreamings, but with earnestness and concentration.*"

Eucharist

After the liturgy of the word, and before we move to the liturgy of the Eucharist, we have a further reminder of our vocation as a chosen race, a royal priesthood, a people set apart. Several persons, representing the entire community, bring bread and wine to the altar. This bread and wine, fruit of the earth and the work of human hands, have been given to us by the Lord of creation as our food and drink. Bringing this food and drink to the altar is a sign that we are now setting them apart from ordinary, daily use for a very special purpose, the worship of God. That action should remind us that we must now set ourselves apart from all our ordinary, everyday activities to do something special, to celebrate the Eucharist.** This does not mean that we should not offer our daily lives in worship to God. We should, for as St. Paul has already reminded us in this Mass, "Whether you eat or drink—whatever you do—you should do all for the glory of God." Every aspect of our lives should be sacred as done for God, but the point is that in the Mass we are engaging in the most significant action of life itself, an act of worship in union with Christ, the purpose of which is to give meaning and value to all the little things we do every

---

** Cf. "Explaining the New Offertory Rite" by Charles E. Miller, C.M. in *The Homiletic and Pastoral Review* for September 1969, pp. 924-927.

day. In the Mass we fulfill our chief duty and express our supreme dignity as a chosen race, a royal priesthood.

The Sacred

The old levitical laws of the Jews concerning ritual uncleanness strike us as odd and unreasonable. Their purpose, however, was to emphasize the sacredness of worship. Certainly we should approach the Mass with an awareness of its sacredness, and we should try to enter into its celebration with as much attention and devotion as possible.

C. E.M.

Seventh Sunday of the Year

WORDS OF FORGIVENESS STILL

We take words for granted. We speak hundreds, perhaps thousands, of words every day without giving very much thought to this human activity. And with our multi-media communications we seem to have accepted the Chinese proverb that one picture is worth a thousand words, but at least in one instance that proverb must be turned around. One word from God is worth more than a thousand pictures. God's word is powerful. It is creative. In the beginning God said, "Let there be light," and there was light. In today's gospel Jesus said, "Your sins are forgiven," and they were forgiven.

Gospel Scene

The setting for the words of Jesus is a memorable scene. When the four friends of the paralytic found it impossible to get through the door to see Jesus, they climbed to the roof with the paralytic on his mat. The roof of this Palestinian house was constructed of beaten earth and twigs or loose flat stones, easily displaced. When the young men had made a large enough hole, they lowered their friend into the room where Jesus stood. Immediately Jesus realized what was expected of him, but he decided first to give the man not what he wanted but what he needed—not a physical cure but a spiritual one. He said simply, "Your sins are forgiven." The scribes were horrified, and their unspoken objection was a good one: "Who can forgive sins except God alone?"

Because Jesus realized what they were thinking, he decided to give a proof of the effectiveness of his words. He posed the question, "Which is easier to say, 'Your sins are forgiven'? or to say, 'Stand up and walk'?" The idea is that you can get away with saying, "Your sins are forgiven." There is no test of whether the words have done anything since no one can see sins in a man's heart. Their being forgiven is invisible. But if you say to a man who cannot walk, "You're cured," everybody can tell in an instant whether the words have produced any result. Jesus did not need to wait for an answer to his question. He declared, "That you may know that the Son of Man has authority on earth to forgive sins" (he said to the paralyzed man), "I command you: Stand up! Pick up your mat and go home." All eyes turned from Jesus to the man lying on his mat. There was a moment of supreme suspense: would he really get up? No doubt bewildered, yet responsive to the words of Jesus, the man rose to his feet, picked up his mat and went outside in the sight of everyone. The people quite understandably were awestruck. They gave praise to God, saying "We have never seen anything like this!" Jesus had made his point: his words were powerful; they accomplished what they signified. With his words he had forgiven the man's sins just as surely as he had cured him of paralysis.

Confession

Jesus forgave the paralytic's sins by his own authority because he was divine. But he did so in a human way, using his voice and tongue and lips to pronounce the words of forgiveness. Those words of forgiveness are with us still, especially in the sacrament of confession. The priest does not forgive sins by his own authority. Were the Church to maintain that he does so, all could reasonably object, "Who can forgive sins except God alone?" In the words of sacramental forgiveness the priest says, "May our Lord Jesus

Seventh Sunday of the Year

Christ absolve you and by his authority I absolve you from your sins in the name of the Father and of the Son and of the Holy Spirit." The words begin with a prayer: "May our Lord Jesus Christ absolve you," and then become a declaration: "*I* absolve you." In that moment of declaration Jesus takes over the voice and tongue and lips of the priest to pronounce the words of absolution. Continuing and extending his incarnation through the priest, Jesus is the one who forgives our sins in confession. He is as present to us as he was to the paralytic.

Faith

The gospel points out that Jesus was moved by the faith of the paralytic and his friends. Climbing the roof indicated that they were determined to let nothing keep them from seeking the help of Jesus in a great need, even if they did not understand what the primary need was. We could do well to imitate their strong faith in our attitude toward confession. Nothing should keep us from seeking the forgiveness of Jesus in this sacrament—not inconvenience, or embarrassment, or dissatisfaction with the minister. Inconvenience? Should we not be willing to climb over every obstacle to seek the forgiveness of Jesus? Embarrassment? How absurd it would have been if the paralytic had objected to his friends, "Don't take me over to that house where Jesus is; everybody will see that I can't walk." All of us are crippled by some sins—that is only human—but how foolish we would be to remain spiritually paralyzed through serious sin only because we are embarrassed at what the priest or others may think of us. Dissatisfaction with the minister? As a priest I am certainly at fault if I am impatient or perfunctory in confession, but remember that in this sacrament you can always receive what you really need: the forgiveness of Jesus Christ.

BREAKING THE BREAD

Invisible

I think we would all appreciate confession a lot more if the effects of sin and forgiveness were not both internal. If the effects of sin were as visible as paralysis and if forgiveness were as obvious as picking up a mat and walking, we very likely would have little trouble placing a great value on the sacrament of confession. Be that as it may, we should seize the opportunity of this Mass to renew our faith in the forgiveness of Jesus Christ and to give praise and thanks to God for a truly wonderful sacrament.

C. E. M.

Eighth Sunday of the Year

THE JOY OF CHRISTIANS

Jesus disturbed people because he was different. He was different from John the Baptist, whom the people had come to respect. John was austere and aloof, but Jesus was relaxed and at ease with every type of person. John preached a fire and brimstone type of sermon, but Jesus preached sermons that were simple and homey, drawn from everyday experiences to which his listeners could easily relate. Jesus was also different from the Pharisees, the religious leaders of the day. The Pharisees had taken all the joy and spirit out of religion by their legalistic approach to man's relationship with God, but Jesus taught a religion of happiness and love.

Question of Fasting

It is not surprising that one day some people objected to Jesus that his disciples did not fast as did the disciples of John and the Pharisees. Jesus answered in a manner typical of him, with a reference to human experience. He said that for his disciples to fast while he was still with them would make as much sense as mourning at a wedding banquet in the presence of the groom. A Jewish wedding banquet was quite a jubilant affair. Remember how important the wine was at the wedding feast of Cana. At a wedding feast the Jews apparently kept in mind one of the psalms which praises God for producing wine from the earth "to gladden men's hearts" (Ps 104:15). Then Jesus admitted that the time would come for fasting when he would be taken away, an allusion to his death.*

* Many scholars maintain that this verse is an addition of the early

61

BREAKING THE BREAD

The Modern Church

Where does that leave us? Is Jesus still with us so that we should not fast, or has he been taken away so that we should fast? The more obvious answer is that Jesus is not with us; he has died and has been taken away into heaven. In a sense that is correct, and so fasting is in order. There will always be a time in the Church for fasting as a sharing in the suffering of Christ until he comes again in glory. Fasting, however, has been de-emphasized in the modern Church partly because of the renewed realization that the resurrected Jesus is indeed still with us, not only in the Eucharist, but in ourselves as members of his Church through baptism. That is why our religion should be one of happiness. It was a jovial monk, Abbot Marmion, the son of an Irish father and a French mother, who wrote, "Joy is the echo of God's life within us."

Marital Union

Moreover, Jesus had entered into a union of deep love with us, not unlike the marriage union. Jesus eminently fulfilled the words of God to his people in our first lesson today: "I will espouse you to myself forever; I will espouse you in love and mercy; I will espouse you in fidelity." It was not without reason that Jesus referred to himself as the bridegroom, a man who wants to share a life of happiness and love with his bride. I suspect that some of you married couples are thinking right now, "Oh, you naive celibate, how little you know about marriage!" Of course every marriage has its ups and downs, but in a good marriage there is even happiness in having someone to share the downs with.

Church to justify its practice of fasting, which found its motivation in the mystery of the cross.

Eighth Sunday of the Year

And the spiritual marriage of Jesus and his people is a good marriage. He is ready to share everything with us because of his deep love, a love of fidelity forever.

Joyful and Generous

Because of this union of love our lives should be characterized by a spirit, not of mourning or sadness, but of joyful and generous love which overflows to others. Maybe you know a couple obviously in love—if you are married, God grant that you are that couple—whose home is always open to anyone. Their mutual love is so great that they seem to have a lot of love left over to share with others. Not only do the parents and the children have many friends, but the whole family without fail is ready and eager to help other people. We as members of the Church must try to realize that the love Christ has given us must overflow, like the miraculous wine at the wedding feast of Cana.

The Mass

Our spirit of joy and love should begin right here in Church. The Mass is not a somber memorial service, conducted by a sorrowful widow. It is a *celebration* of the death of Christ, with all the spirit of jubilation which the word "celebration" suggests. We do not mourn over the death of Christ, for we see it in the light of his resurrection and with a realization that it was through his death that Jesus espoused us to himself. Our celebration is enhanced, not with food and wine, however elegant and exquisite, but with the body and blood of Christ. Jesus again proclaims: "This is my body which is given up for you. This is my blood, the blood of the new and everlasting covenant." That covenant is the marriage covenant, effecting our union with Jesus.

Yes, Jesus is still with us and he wants his joy and love

BREAKING THE BREAD

to spread from our hearts and through our hands. Let all the world look at us and see that we are different, as different as Jesus was, and let all the world say, "Those Catholics are a happy and joyful lot."

C. E. M.

Ninth Sunday of the Year
Suggested Use: Third Eucharistic Prayer

"I DON'T GO TO CHURCH ANY MORE"

What do you do when your son stops going to Mass? Or your daughter? Or both? Do you simply put your foot down and say, "As long as you're under our roof you are going to Mass"? But does that really answer the question your son or daughter is silently asking? Or you may take another route: "After all the money we've spent on your Catholic education, and all the other sacrifices we've made for you, this is what we get out of it, an irreligious child?" Again, no one in his right mind can deny the sacrifices Catholic parents have made to support our parochial grade and high schools as well as C.C.D. programs, but does your statement about sacrifices answer the unspoken question in your child's mind? And even if you decide that it's up to your boy or girl to make his or her own decision about going to church, your position still does not answer the question that is troubling them.

The Question

The question that needs answering is not from parents to children: "Why don't you go to Mass any more?" Rather it is from child to parent, "Why do you go to Mass every Sunday?" You may think that your answer is obvious, that your good example over all these years should be sufficient answer in itself. Obviously if you did not think it important, you would not have made the effort to get yourself and your family to Sunday Mass. After all, there have been many days when you did not feel like going, but you went anyway. And what about those days during vacation when you went miles out of your way to find a church? Don't these efforts say

BREAKING THE BREAD

anything at all about why you go to Mass? Don't they shout out that Sunday Mass is the most important thing in the week? But the gnawing question is still there, "Why?"

First Reading

The readings in today's Mass give us some clues for answering the question. At first glance the reading from the Old Testament seems to reinforce the statement, "You go to Mass because I tell you to go." "Take care to keep holy the sabbath day as the Lord, your God, commanded you." However, as we read to the end of the section we find that God gives not only the command, but also a reason for it. God recalls to the minds of the people for whom this law was written that they were once slaves and he brought them out of captivity. "This is why the Lord, your God, has commanded you to observe the sabbath day." The release from the slavery of the Egyptians was not a negative gift, but God's positive way of establishing the Israelites as the Chosen People. Because their freedom from the Egyptians was such a grand thing, the Hebrew people were commanded by God not to forget it. And the remembrance was to be kept alive by setting aside one day each week to recall such a magnificent benefit.

Gratitude

We go to Mass because God tells us to go, but there is a reason behind the commandment—a reason we can see only if we have faith. It all really comes down to that—faith that because God has created us we belong entirely to him, faith that Jesus has saved us from the eternal death of sin, faith that in our baptism God granted us freedom from the slavery of sin and made us his new Chosen People.

Ninth Sunday of the Year

The second reading today can give us some good insights into the significance of our baptism. God has shone his light in our hearts, "that we in turn might make known the glory of God shining on the face of Christ." By baptism such a close relationship with God was established that we can act in the person of his son, Jesus Christ. In fact it is true to say that Christ does not fulfill his redemption of mankind except through us. "While we live we are constantly being delivered to death for Jesus' sake, so that the life of Jesus may be revealed in our mortal flesh." Nowhere is this more perfectly accomplished than in the Mass. If we are going to be true to our heritage in baptism, then the Mass becomes an integral part of our lives. We are the people about whom the Third Eucharistic Prayer is speaking when it says, "From age to age you gather a people to yourself, so that from east to west a perfect offering may be made to the glory of your name."

Participation

Parents who realize the necessity for harmonious action among all the members of the family if all are going to benefit, should be able to see also the necessity for God to gather his people to himself, at least once a week. It is when we come together as a group of people who believe in the same God, who have each benefited by the redemption of his son, who are all inspired by the Holy Spirit, that we can fulfill the words we proclaim in the preface: "It is right to give him thanks and praise." We should not come to church out of fear that something terrible will happen to us if we don't; rather we should wish to join with Christ and all those called together here to praise God our Father for his wonderful benefits to us. Hopefully too the spirit of love and generosity gene-

BREAKING THE BREAD

rated while we are participating in the Mass will flow over into our daily lives, "so that the life of Jesus may be revealed in our mortal flesh."

Beginnings of an Answer

When we have struggled sufficiently with the question, "Why go to Mass?", we will find that it really does all come down to a question of faith. In the final analysis we go to Mass because we believe in God and in what he has done for us. We believe in Jesus Christ who in the gospel for today proclaims himself "Lord of the sabbath." We believe in his words, "This is my body...this is my blood...do this in memory of me."

O. J. M.

Recommended reading: "What Do You Do When Your Son Stops Going to Mass?" an article in *St. Anthony Messenger* for August 1971 by Dolores Curran.

First Sunday of Lent

THE CHRISTIAN RAINBOW

Parents like to tell their children, even their adult children, about things that happened to them when they were infants. Many a child has heard more than once about his being lost for several hours and making everyone frantic, including the neighbors, or about how he would always want to climb into bed with his parents during a thunderstorm. Most of us tend to discount the experiences of our earliest days, not only because the stories are usually embarrassing, but also because we have to take events of our infancy on the word of others since, of course, we have no personal memory of them. But I think another reason is that for the most part we feel that only little things happened to us when we were little people. Psychologists, however, generally insist that all the things we have experienced, no matter at how early an age, have had their impact. Their mark is on us.

Baptism

On this first Sunday of Lent the Church, like an interested and concerned parent, wants to remind us of something that happened to most of us when we were infants, something wonderful and momentous, and that something is our baptism. No matter how little we were, it was a very big thing. But whether we were baptized as infants or later in life, we have to take the significance of that event on the word of the Church as she teaches us God's revelation concerning the importance of this sacrament, an importance we must not discount.

The great value of baptism is that it communicates to us

the saving grace of Jesus Christ. To help us appreciate this meaning of baptism, St. Peter (second lesson) teaches us that the rescue of Noah from the flood was a prefigurement of baptism. In baptism God extends his hand to rescue us from the flood of human misery, to save us from drowning in the engulfing waters of sin. Moreover, after God had saved Noah from the flood, he made the rainbow a symbol of his mercy and love. A rainbow is a sign that the storm is over, that the danger has passed. Baptism is the Christian rainbow. Even after our baptism we will continue to see clouds of evil gathering all around us. We will still hear the distant rumbling of a hatred that wishes to destroy us. But our baptism should make us realize that we need not fear the threatening thunderstorms of life. Baptism is the symbol of God's mercy and love, the sign that he will not allow a flood of hatred and evil to destroy us.

Lent and Baptism

According to a very ancient custom the Church has always emphasized the sacrament of baptism during Lent. Originally the catechumens, those who were seeking baptism, were required to spend the entire season of Lent preparing to receive this sacrament on Holy Saturday. Now of course infants and even adults are baptized throughout the year. And yet the Church does not want us to abandon the traditional spirit of Lent. That is why at the conclusion of Lent we will all be invited to renew our baptismal promises, either within the Holy Saturday liturgy or during the Mass of Easter Sunday.

Notice that the Church will invite us to *renew* our baptismal promises. What are we expected to renew? What did we promise through our godparents or even personally if we were adults? According to St. Peter (second reading) the basic promise or pledge is a good conscience. Baptism is a

First Sunday of Lent

covenant, an agreement between God and us. God promised his mercy and love, and we promised a life of fidelity. He became our God and we became his people. If our renewal of baptism is not to be merely an empty gesture, we must spend the time of Lent seriously considering our relationship with God. Jesus in the gospel says: "Reform your lives." That is a message the Church continues to preach to all of us without exception. It means that we must have the courage to work at changing whatever needs to be changed about our way of living. Lent should be devoted to an honest appraisal of what we are doing with our time and with our talents. That appraisal is something each one of us must make for himself. No one can do it for us.

Penance

During Lent the official forms of penance have been greatly reduced (in the United States). Only Ash Wednesday and Good Friday are days of fast and abstinence. Catholics who are fourteen years of age and older are asked to abstain from meat on the Fridays of Lent. This simple penance should remind us that we must turn away from selfishness and turn our minds and hearts to God by striving to be more earnest in prayer. It should also remind us that we must overcome any smallness which prevents us from being considerate of others and generous in works of charity.

Mark and Sign

As we look into ourselves to see how we have given in to evil through selfishness and smallness and how we have shared in hatred through our failure to love God and others as Jesus has taught us, we should never be discouraged. In the covenant of baptism God has promised that evil and hatred

BREAKING THE BREAD

will not destroy us; he has given us a pledge of his mercy and love. One of these days after a Spring rain, we may have the good fortune of seeing a rainbow in the sky. It is the sign of God's covenant with us.

C. E. M.

Second Sunday of Lent

A HINT OF GLORY

Pagan people before the time of Christ thought of their gods as divine beings who had to be paid or even bribed for their help in human affairs. In time of great national distress some people even sacrificed a first-born son with the idea that nothing was too good for the gods. They hoped that their gods could not fail to respond to such a sacrifice. Barbaric though the act was, there was a certain heroism about it. Since Abraham, the father of the chosen people, felt compelled to show no less a heroism than his pagan neighbors, he prepared to sacrifice his son Isaac to the one true God. Abraham's intention manifested a special heroism. God had promised Abraham that he would establish his covenant with him and his descendants and that he would make him the father of a multitude of nations (Gn 17:4, 7). Abraham understood that all of God's promises would be fulfilled through Isaac. It was terrible enough to be asked to sacrifice his son. What disturbed him the more was that the death of his young child would seem to render God's promises impossible of fulfillment. The whole idea seemed absurd, something that did not appear to make sense. Abraham was heroic not only in his generosity but in his trust in God as well.

His Own Son

God was pleased with Abraham's good will, but today's first reading indicates that while his people had to be prepared to give up everything, even their most precious possessions, God did not require human sacrifice. He himself provided a ram in place of the first-born son.* And yet what God did not require of his people he did require of himself. We have become so used to the idea of the crucifixion of the Son of God that we are not sufficiently impressed by this sacrifice. St. Paul, however, never stopped reflecting on this great mystery. Fully aware of the Abraham-Isaac incident, he wrote to the Romans: "God did not spare his own Son but handed him over for the sake of us all" (second reading).

Shock and Dismay

St. Paul of course reflected on the meaning of the cross in the light of the resurrection. He was impressed with the magnanimity of God's act, but since he clearly understood that the obedient death of Jesus led directly to his glorification, he did not see the cross as either barbaric or absurd (1 Cor 1:23f). Such was not the case for the apostles who before the resurrection heard Jesus himself predict that he would have to suffer and die on a cross. They were understandably shocked to think that their master would have to undergo so horrible a fate. They were also dismayed because they hoped that Jesus would set Israel free, something they believed a dead leader could not accomplish. The apostles lacked both the generosity and the complete trust of Abraham.

Resurrection Foreshadowed

Jesus saw the shock and dismay of his apostles. He knew what a trial his passion and death would be for them. And so it was that six days after he had made the prediction of his crucifixion he took Peter, James, and John up a high mountain where he was transfigured before them The magni-

---

* Cf. *A New Look at an Old Book* by Luke H. Grollenberg, pp. 37f.

ficent change that came over his physical appearance was a preview of the glory of his resurrection. Though the transfiguration was really little more than a hint of the glory that would come to Jesus through his death, it was intended to bolster the faith and trust of the apostles, to prepare them for the ordeal of the passion.

Death and Glory

During Lent we ought to think more about the sacrifice of the cross. We should try to appreciate God's love for us by considering that he did not spare his own Son but handed him over for the sake of us all. But we must also realize that for Jesus suffering and death led to glory and happiness. Most important of all we should see that Jesus made the passage through death to eternal life for our sake, so that he might raise us from death to a life of glory and happiness. The transfiguration, together with its fulfillment in the resurrection, is a sign of our own future glory as God's beloved children.

What would life be without God's love for us? Some have thought that human existence is nothing more than a struggle for survival so that we may live some seventy or eighty years with pain and suffering most of the time. For them life is little better than the barbarism of the jungle. Others have judged that life is only a vain search for a drop of temporal happiness amid a torrent of frustration and sorrow, with death at the end as a welcome oblivion. For them life is absurd. How different should be our outlook as Christians! In the words of today's responsorial psalm we must believe even amid the greatest afflictions that we are precious in the eyes of God, and that one day we will walk in his presence forever.

Let us make of this Mass a sacrifice of thanksgiving to God for having given us a hint of the glory and happiness

BREAKING THE BREAD

that will one day be ours, a glory and happiness that will come to us because God did not spare his own Son but handed him over for the sake of us all.

C. E. M.

Third Sunday of Lent

TRUE WORSHIP

Gift giving has become a rather prominent aspect of our society. In addition to the Christian custom, we give gifts for birthdays, anniversaries, graduations, weddings, mother's day and father's day. In all of this the economic factor plays no little part because gift giving makes for good business. Every now and then we voice a complaint about how commercialized it has all become, but more importantly we should be concerned about the meaning of gift giving. There must be something behind the gift because giving a gift is a way of saying something. A husband's gift to his wife on their wedding anniversary, no matter how costly, may have no real significance. The gift should mean that she is first in his affection, but if he is unfaithful to her, the gift is hollow and hypocritical. Any wife worthy of her womanhood wants her husband, not just some meaningless present. A gift is symbolic; to be acceptable, it must represent the giver.

The Temple

Sacrifice is a form of worship which involves gift giving. When Jesus cleared the temple in Jerusalem of the merchants and their animals, he showed how upset he was that sacrifice there had become commercialized. He complained, "Stop turning my Father's house into a marketplace." Actually the buying and selling of animals to be used in the temple sacrifice was legitimate in the temple precincts, the outer courtyards surrounding the holy places, and was originally intended as a convenience, especially for non-residents of Jerusalem who could hardly have been expected to bring oxen, sheep, or doves with them when they had to travel a long distance to get to the city. What Jesus really objected to was the fact that for both buyers and sellers the whole transaction had become devoid of the spirit of worship. For the merchants it was simply a sure way to make money. For the customers the purchase of an animal was the prelude to what had degenerated for many into an empty ritual, something they did merely because it was expected of them.

The Commandments

In the time of Jesus many Jews had forgotten the nature of their calling as the chosen people. The Lord had declared that he would be their God and they would be his people. The Israelites were to be the worshippers of the one true God, who said to them: "I, the Lord am your God. You shall not have other gods besides me." According to God's directions part of worship was the offering of animal sacrifices. That offering was a form of gift giving. There was nothing practical about the offering in the sense that God certainly did not need oxen or sheep or doves. The offerings were to be symbolic of the affection and loyalty of the people. Sacrifice had to be backed up by a life of loving obedience to God. That is why when God stated that he alone was to be worshipped, at the same time he also gave the ten commandments to his people. Following the commandments was to be a concrete way of living out the meaning of worship.

A New Sacrifice

Jesus condemned a worship which had become commercialized and largely hypocritical. But he did not stop there. He fully intended to replace it with a perfect form of wor-

Third Sunday of Lent

ship, the sacrifice of himself on the cross. When the temple officials demanded a sign for his authority, Jesus responded, "Destroy this temple and in three days I will raise it up." The statement was admittedly obscure to the officials, but St. John explains for us that Jesus was referring to the temple of his body. It was an apt figure of speech. The inadequate worship of the temple would find perfection in the sacrifice of Jesus, the true temple of God. The animal offerings of Judaism would be replaced by the self-oblation of the Son of God in his death and resurrection.*

New Chosen People

As Catholics we are the new chosen people of God. God has called us to be his true worshippers, and in the Mass he himself has provided us with a perfect sacrificial gift, not oxen or sheep or doves, but the body and blood of his own Son. The Mass is more excellent than the Old Testament sacrifices in the degree that Jesus Christ is more excellent than irrational animals. That is a truth we must always keep in mind when we enter this church, this temple of God. But above all we must remember that the Mass is a form of gift giving. It must be expressive of our affection, our loyalty, our faithfulness to God. We certainly should try to make our participation in Mass enthusiastic and devout, but the measure of our sincerity will be found in how we live. It really does little good to give God a gift with one hand in the Mass and to take it back with the other hand in daily conduct.

Our Worship

Jesus first lived a life of loving obedience to his heavenly Father, and then made the offering of himself on the cross.

* For a rather complete treatment of today's gospel, cf. *The Gospel of St. John* by John Marsh in the Pelican Gospel Commentaries series.

BREAKING THE BREAD

He needed only one offering because he did it perfectly once and for all. We come to Mass to make a promise that we will live lives of loving obedience, and then we have to try to fulfill that promise. Of course we never make a perfect offering nor do we keep our promise completely. That is why God continually gives us the opportunity to renew our offering in every Mass, and to make a new start at keeping our promise as we leave this temple of worship. The important thing is that we never stop trying, despite our failures. God indeed is well aware of what is in our heart, and he wants to see there a reflection of the worship we offer him in the Mass.

C. E. M.

Fourth Sunday of Lent

GOD SO LOVED THE WORLD

A play called *Inherit the Wind* was made into a movie starring Spencer Tracy and Frederick March. Every now and then the movie is shown on television, and perhaps you have seen it. The plot revolves around the true story of a high school instructor by the name of John Scopes who in 1925 violated an old law of Tennessee by teaching evolution in his high school biology class. Among other things, John Scopes was accused of having said: "God made man in his own image and likeness and man returned the compliment." The implication was that man had dragged God down to his own level by attributing to him human characteristics.

Contrast

Whether John Scopes ever really made that statement is uncertain, but its implication is true regarding many religions. It is only natural for people groping to understand God to think of him in anthropomorphic terms. Ancient pagans especially thought of their gods as being ambitious, jealous, even lustful. In opposition to their neighbors the Israelites of the Old Testament maintained a faith in one true God, a transcendent being prior to and exalted above the universe, spiritual and perfect in every way. They arrived at this notion, not through natural groping, but through supernatural revelation from God himself. Of course that revelation was necessarily expressed in human words and in reference to human traits, but far from presenting a god in the likeness of man, that revelation formed an image of God by means of contrast with human imperfections. Where man was small

BREAKING THE BREAD

and petty, God was big and generous. Where man was vindictive and hateful, God was forgiving and loving.

Old Testament

Here is an example of the contrast between God and human beings. For human beings there is always a limit to endurance, the last straw. A husband or wife may forgive a single infidelity on the part of a spouse, but repeated affairs are more than anyone can put up with. Not so with God. God looked upon his chosen people as his spouse, but in spite of their repeated infidelities he never gave up on them. In fact the Old Testament is largely a story of the almost incredible patience of God. Today's first lesson is a good example. It was written about three hundred years before Christ when the author could look back on a long history in which the people "added infidelity to infidelity." And yet he saw that "early and often did the Lord, the God of their fathers, send his messengers to them, for he had compassion on his people...." The author also interpreted punishments from God as vindictive but as truly medicinal, designed to cure the people of the sickness of sin. God's patience and love were much more than anything that could be expected of a human being.

New Testament

But it took the New Testament revelation in Jesus Christ to bring out how much God really loves the world. Today's gospel illustrates the advance made by New Testament revelation by reference to an incident recorded in the Old Testament book of Numbers. Trying to enter directly into Palestine from the South after the exodus from Egypt, the Israelites found the way blocked and had to skirt Edom so as to

Fourth Sunday of Lent

come in from the East. The people were not happy about the detour and grumbled against God and Moses. God punished the people by sending poisonous snakes among them. Then in his mercy he commanded Moses to make a bronze serpent and erect it as a standard. The people were saved by turning in faith toward the bronze serpent lifted up by Moses. Jesus himself saw in the lifting up of the serpent a type or sign of his own lifting up on the cross. That is why today's gospel quotes Jesus as saying, "Just as Moses lifted up the serpent in the desert, so must the Son of man be lifted up, that all who believe may have eternal life in him." Then St. John comments, "Yes, God so loved the world that he gave his only Son." All through the Old Testament God had shown his love through men like Moses and by means of merciful incidents like that of the bronze serpent. But in the fullness of time God manifested even greater love in the degree that Jesus is greater than Moses and to the extent that his being lifted up on the cross is greater than the lifting up of the bronze serpent in the desert.

St. Paul

St. Paul, a man steeped in the Old Testament, was almost overwhelmed with the magnitude of God's love as shown in Jesus Christ. It is no wonder that in today's second lesson, almost in ecstasy, he cried out: "God is rich in mercy; because of his great love for us he brought us to life with Christ when we were dead in sin. By this favor you were saved." Despite a long history of human perversity, "God did not send his Son into the world to condemn the world, but that the world might be saved through him." That kind of love is beyond human imagining. And God does not change. He still has that kind of love for us.

BREAKING THE BREAD

True Image

Some of us at times may think that this picture of God makes him out to be too soft or weak. Perhaps the problem is that deep down we know that we ourselves cannot even begin to be as patient and forgiving as God is. Though we would like to be unselfish and generous we realize that our love for others does not come anywhere near the kind of love God has for us. Subconsciously we fall into the mistake of trying to make God in our own image and likeness. We can begin to have an idea of God's love, not by looking at ourselves, but by turning in faith toward the image of Jesus Christ lifted up on the cross.

C. E. M.

Fifth Sunday of Lent
Suggested use: eucharistic acclamation B

A LAW OF LIFE

Within Sequoia National Park in California towers the famous General Sherman redwood tree, three hundred and sixty-five feet tall. The tree is so tall that if you were to stand as much as thirty feet away and try to see the top you would fall over backwards. At its base rests a plaque containing a seed taken from the tree, a seed no larger than the nail on your little finger. A similar seed, buried in the earth, needed sun, water, soil and about twenty-five centuries to grow to the present height of three hundred and sixty-five feet.

Grain of Wheat

This tree in America was approximately five centuries old when Jesus walked the earth in far-off Palestine. At that time it was slowly but persistently growing heavenward, a living example of the mysterious words of Jesus in today's gospel: "Unless the grain of wheat falls to the earth and dies, it remains just a grain of wheat. But if it dies, it produces much fruit." With these words Jesus proclaimed the paradox of the Father's plan, that death is the source of life. It is a law of sacrifice, that one can come to a greater life only by dying to a lesser one. It is a law exemplified in nature—in a grain of wheat and in the seed of a tree. A seed which does not "die" by being buried in the earth can never grow into something greater. Jesus was like a seed. He had to die and be buried in the earth for three days. Then on Easter Sunday he pushed through the soil, like a growing tree, and reached heaven to enjoy the fullness of new life.

BREAKING THE BREAD

Obedience

Today's second lesson from the letter to the Hebrews presents the same law of sacrifice, though less graphically. However, it emphasizes that accepting the law was not easy for Jesus, who, though divine, was also as human as we are in all things but sin. The author reminds us that Jesus prayed with tears to be saved from death. We have only to think of Jesus in the garden of Gethsemane to feel the full force of these words. Difficult though it was to embrace death, Jesus did so in loving obedience to his Father. Ironically through his obedience Jesus was indeed saved from death, not in the sense that he did not have to die at all, but in the sense that through his resurrection he overcame the effects of death as he rose to a new, glorified life.

For Our Sake

Jesus accepted death in obedience to his father for our sake. He made the passage through death before us to take away the effects of eternal death. Through his exaltation in the resurrection he became the source of eternal salvation for all who accept him. Jesus said in the gospel, "And I—once I am lifted up from the earth—will draw all men to myself." The phrase, to be lifted up, has a double meaning. It refers to his being lifted up on the cross in death and to his being lifted up to life in the resurrection. Jesus wishes to draw us to himself to share in his death so that we may also share in his resurrection.

Spanning the Centuries

Jesus lived and died at a definite point in time, and yet he spans the centuries before and after his sojourn on this earth. He was planted like a seed in Old Testament times, a

Easter Sunday

seed of hope. Today's first lesson is almost a summary of the entire Old Testament. Again and again God offered a covenant to his people, a pledge of his salvation in return for their obedience. Even as his people broke the covenant by disobedience, God through the prophets taught them to hope for salvation, for a new covenant in which God would forgive sin. That hope of the new covenant was realized in Jesus Christ, and sealed in his blood, "the blood of the new and everlasting covenant."

And Jesus still lives today. He stands like a giant redwood, reaching heavenward toward our eternal destiny. Face death we must; it is inevitable. We cannot escape death, but we can overcome it in union with Jesus. He is the only way to salvation. Wherever we go, whatever we do, we will find no answer to the problem of death and sin other than Jesus himself.

Faith

In the eucharistic acclamation today we will proclaim our faith in Jesus: "Dying you destroyed our death; rising you restored our life; Lord Jesus, come in glory." That proclamation is an expression of our belief that, no matter how small or insignificant we may seem, we can grow with Jesus to the fullness of everlasting life.

C. E. M.

Passion Sunday
(Palm Sunday)

CHEERS AND BOOS

Professional ballplayers know what it is to hear both cheers and boos from a crowd. A shortstop may be hailed as a hero one day when he makes brilliant plays and goes three for four at the plate, and the next day he may be treated as a bum when he makes two crucial errors and fails to get even one hit. It is no surprise when a player complains that fans are fickle and have short memories. And of course he sees his opponents saddened by his success and delighted by his failure.

Reactions

In his life Jesus was playing no game. His work was supremely serious. During his public ministry he cured those with bodily ills in anticipation of his sacrifice whereby he would heal people of the spiritual sickness of sin. He fed the hungry as a sign of the spiritual nourishment he would give in his own body and blood. These physical favors aroused the enthusiasm of the crowds, an enthusiasm which reached a fever pitch in the cheers and "hosannas" of Palm Sunday. His enemies were indeed saddened by his apparent success with the crowds, but Jesus knew that his hero's welcome would be short-lived. On Good Friday the cheers and "hosannas" were changed to boos and taunts to the delight of his opponents.

Anticipation

Jesus knew how people would react to his apparent failure on Good Friday. He tried to anticipate that reaction by teaching them that his death was a necessity for their salvation. During Lent in the gospels we have heard how he taught that he had to be lifted up on the cross, that he was to be like a grain of wheat buried in the earth, and that when the temple of his body was destroyed he would raise it up on the third day. To three of his apostles he gave the magnificent sign of his transfiguration. But the human memory is short, and the human heart is fickle. When Jesus was taken into custody, his apostles ran away in fear. When he was lifted up on the cross, the people jeered at him. When he was buried, his enemies thought it was the end of him. Admittedly Good Friday was a bleak day for anyone who had put his hope in Jesus.

Our King

Today we are asked to hail Christ as our King, our hero. But we must remember that Christ's victory came only through the cross. That is why on this day, even as we celebrate Christ's triumphant procession into Jerusalem, the Church gives us in this Mass the account of his passion and death. And in the reading from the letter to the Philippians St. Paul summarizes the whole meaning of Holy Week and Easter: "He humbled himself, obediently accepting even death, death on a cross! Because of this, God highly exalted him . . . ."

St. Paul also gives a summary of Christian living: "Your attitude must be Christ's attitude." To be a follower of Christ we must accept with loving obedience whatever comes from the hand of God, including death itself. That is the only way to true happiness. Let us pray that our memories will not be so short that we forget this lesson when the time comes for us to share in the passion of Christ. Let us pray that we will not be so fickle as to accept Christ as our King when

BREAKING THE BREAD

all is going well, only to reject him when we are faced with human suffering.

We do not read the account of the passion and death of Christ while forgetting how it all turns out in his resurrection from the dead. Nor should we forget that all of the bleak Good Fridays of our lives will lead to glorious resurrection in an eternal Easter Sunday.

C. E. M.

Easter Sunday

SUPERSTAR!

Easter Sunday totally reverses the image of Good Friday. On Good Friday Jesus Christ did not look anything like a superstar. No doubt people standing around the cross looked up at him and said, "He's a man; he's just a man."

Perspective

Easter Sunday puts everything about Jesus into perspective and tells us what Good Friday was all about. It shows that what really happened on Good Friday was not an execution but a sacrifice, not a defeat but a triumph, not an end but a beginning. The death of Jesus was not an execution because no force, human or otherwise, had the power to kill Jesus. He freely accepted death in loving obedience to the will of his heavenly Father, as a sacrificial offering of himself for the salvation of the world. His death was not a defeat. Rather it was a great triumph over the twin enemies of the human race, sin and death. His death was not an end, for Jesus made of death a passage to a higher, better life. He has gone before us in death to show us the way through the darkness of the tomb to the brilliant light of resurrection, the beginning of the fullness of life to which we are all called in the sacrament of baptism, which we will renew this day.

Two Feasts

I believe that most of us tend to put Christmas and Easter together. We look upon these two days as the two feasts of the Church which mean the most to us. They are alike and yet different. At Christmas we celebrate a beginning in the birth of Jesus. Even though Jesus really began his human life nine months earlier at the time of his conception, we think of his birth as the beginning of his human life. In his birth, Jesus came to us, human like us in all things but sin. At Easter we also celebrate a beginning. It was the beginning of a fuller life, for Jesus did not rise from the dead merely to continue the life he had led on this earth for some thirty years. He rose to a glorified life of perfect happiness wherein he put behind him all the suffering and misery and tears that are our human lot. At Easter, in one sense, Jesus left us behind, but he wishes to draw us to himself so that we may share in his glorified life forever.

Easter Egg

Christmas is of course much more appealing to us with all its decorations, its wonderful carols, and its spirit of gift-giving. Easter is almost stark in comparison. There is one simple symbol of Easter which we should think about, however, and that is the Easter egg. Originally when the Lenten fast was extremely strict in the early Church, eggs were forbidden food. It was only natural then that on Easter Sunday people wanted to enjoy this food from which they had abstained during the long period of Lent. An egg, however, is an excellent symbol of the meaning of Easter for Jesus as well as for ourselves. Within a fertilized egg life is slowly unfolding. When the time for hatching arrives, the chick emerges from the shell to begin a full, free life as Jesus emerged from the tomb to a glorified life. Right now we are living a very confined life, like that of a chick within its shell. We hope that one day we will break the shell of this life to be free to live with Jesus his glorified life. The bright colors with which we dye Easter eggs are a sign of our joy over Christ's resurrection and the expectation of our own.

Easter Sunday

Superstar

Easter reverses the image of Good Friday. It shows that Jesus Christ is truly a Superstar who will lead us one day to the happiness of eternal life in heaven.

C. E. M.

Second Sunday of Easter

FAITH POWER THROUGH FORGIVENESS

Stories coming out of wartime concentration camps in Germany and Poland are full of insights of man at his best. Fr. Maximilian Kolbe turned a starvation block into a house of prayer. Sr. Benedicta (Gertrude Stein) turned agnostics into believers. Common suffering seems to have forced common concern for each other. Sharing of food, caring for one another, forgiving offenses, occurred almost as Luke describes in the early Christian community.

But the most amazing aspect was the power some had to sustain their own life. Dr. Viktor Frankl suggests that certain "dying" victims had a vision of what they had to do when they got out. A child, husband, wife, parents, a neglected friend, someone—was waiting for them. They had faith that they were needed to settle a family feud, to apologize to a neighbor, and would get out. This faith to love and forgive was a power which enabled them to survive.

Faith Power

St. Luke suggests in the first reading that the apostles bore witness "with power." The power they had was their faith in the risen Christ and the power to forgive sins. It was this force that allowed the early Christians to become one, to have unity and to survive under persecution.

The Christian community and their Old Testament ancestors were impressed with the symbols of water and blood. Both are signs of life: water in the desert and the waters of Baptism; and the blood of Christ on the cross and the blood of the Eucharist giving life. Christ not only suffered the water bath of Baptism but came through the blood bath of the crucifixion.

Ourselves

We could apply this to ourselves and suggest that if we want to have unity and forgiveness not only do we have to offer a cup of water to the least friend, but we have to be willing to offer our life. Christ has already given us "power" in Baptism and the Eucharist. He has shown us how to forgive in confession. So why don't we believe strongly? Why don't we forgive freely?

Our problem is: we haven't seen, so we don't have a strong faith power. If Christ stood here before us and invited us by name to investigate his wounds, maybe we would have Faith. But we haven't seen, so we can't be like the apostles; nor have we suffered together in persecution. We have no bond of concern for each other. We don't forgive. So when the risen Lord imparts his blessing of peace through the person next to us, we're not ready. We're suspicious of the others or we just don't care.

Solution

As bad as it sounds there is room for a solution, if we admit that we suffer from time to time, and recognize that everyone has problems. And if we can say we all are suffering together, and this has meaning in the light of Christ's suffering, we might be willing to forgive each other. After all, we're in the same boat and the same storm. Then we would be open to be "begotten by God" and to be given a stronger faith.

It's not surprising that ecumenism is farthest advanced

in the European areas that suffered the most during the second world war.

Recognizing that we suffer together leads to great forgiveness and concern. Being filled with caring allows God to be present and gives us stronger faith which helps us to survive the suffering itself. "The power that has conquered the world (of problems and suffering) is this faith of ours."

We are blessed because even though we haven't seen the risen Christ, we have experienced his forgiveness in the sacrament of Penance and in the greeting of peace. His love flows through us in Baptism and the Eucharist (water and blood). The Lord knows we are not the greatest lovers and forgivers. We might not get close to being a Kolbe or Stein. But we have a lot to be proud of: we will try and the Lord will call us blessed because we have not seen, but believe.

M. M. R.

Third Sunday of Easter

THE LEAST LIKELY IS THE BEST BET

Just before the turn of the century, a train rumbled through a French province headed for Paris. Two men sat opposite each other: the one a young soldier obviously bored with the inactivity, the other an old man quite content to quietly finger his rosary beads. As the monotonous miles bumped along, the soldier could restrain himself no longer. He blurted out in the direction of the old man: "God isn't going to save our world, science is!" The old man merely smiled and nodded, continuing to move the next bead through his fingers. The "put down" was too much of a challenge to avoid, so the young man launched into a tirade on the marvels of science in business and medicine. Declaring religion to be dying out as the light of science came in, he continued his attack until the train came into the Paris depot. As the youth stood up to get his bag, he felt sorry for the old man—silently taking the abuse for the past hour. Trying to sound a bit kinder, he introduced himself. The ancient one shook the soldier's hand and reached into his vest for a card. The youngster accepted the card and helped the old man down the step. Then he glanced at the card: "Dr. Louis Pasteur, Academy of Science, Paris."

No Faith

All of us are surprised when the least expected person turns out to be the expert and produces the right answers. An inmate behind the fence of the mental institution watched a man outside standing by his car, after kids had run off with

BREAKING THE BREAD

the bolts to one of his tires. "Take one bolt from each of the other tires and use them to hold that one until you get to a gas station." "That's a fine idea. What are you doing in there?" "Well, I may be insane, but I'm not stupid." We just don't have faith in certain people. We sell them short. The disciples on the road to Emmaus couldn't "see" Christ because they were convinced he was still dead. Mary Magdalene was the same. She could not see Christ in the garden because she didn't look through the eyes of faith: faith in the risen Lord. And the disciples were terribly disturbed by a "ghost" because they were convinced Christ had died for good.

A lot of us suffer from this myopic vision. We fail to look for the right things in the right places. We don't believe what our eyes see. We have to gear our sights wider to the least expected carriers of grace, or continue to miss out. How many friends have we only superficially appreciated because we see no value in them? How often do we fail to read, or study to find out about public issues, simply because we know we're right, or "all politicians speak the same way?" When is the last time you seriously listened to a "little kid?" How can we possibly grow wiser if we don't listen and search?

Vision of Christ

The same applies even more to our vision of Christ. If we only have faith in a remote god-creator who somehow keeps the world going, then we will not see and experience the God-man Christ who knows our problems, walks with us, accepts us for the way we are. We won't grow. We won't know what a Pentecostal is talking about. To "experience" the divine presence of Jesus is just too emotional for us. If Jesus Christ asked for a bite of our fish—he couldn't be God. He's too common, too available.

Third Sunday of Easter

Practice Makes Perfect

As Peter suggests, we can "put to death the author of life" by our ignorance. If we don't have faith in the risen, loving Lord—he's as good as dead for us.

How do I know I have the right faith-vision of Christ? John answers: "The way we can be sure of our knowledge of him is to keep his commandments." Love others as I have loved you. At rock bottom this means appreciating those we think little of. Then we should start "acting" like Christ is right along side of us. Talk to him during the day and share events. If we really get good at this practicing, soon the reality will dawn on us. The power of Christ will move over us with "sheer joy and wonder." And we will begin to know that "God raised him from the dead, and we are his witnesses." Then the peace and joy of the apostles will be ours. And we will want to spread the good News. Maybe even begin when you turn to the one next to you and proclaim: "The Lord is risen, peace be with you."

M. M. R.

Fourth Sunday of Easter

INVEST IN THIS STOCK

Anyone who works for a living (unless he is self-employed) is very impressed with a kind employer. Most employees brag about it: "I have a tremendous boss. He only blows up when I make big mistakes." Or better, we brag about a superintendent who just happens to be a friend of ours.

The secret of Christ's early success was probably something like this. Simple people recognized Christ as a strong leader. But they also were flattered because this strong leader liked them, and he didn't get too upset when they missed the point. And we have a right to feel the same way. In spite of our frequent failings, Christ loves us. How much more flattering when we realize that Christ reflects the Father, the great God of thunderous creation who happens to like us. And more, he wants us not just to work for him but to join the family. Yet what else could we expect from a loving father who calls us his children? The kinder Christ was to his friends the more they could marvel at and praise the father: "our dear Abba."

Why Rejected?

This is probably the reason it's so hard to understand why the Jewish people of Christ's time rejected him. We can understand a stone being carelessly set aside by ignorant builders, but not the living shepherd being rejected by his flock. It's like a doctor being dumped by his patients, or a mother abandoned by her children. Yet Christ didn't satisfy, or better, didn't qualify for what the Jewish people felt they needed. His kindness as a leader was wasted on them. His

Fourth Sunday of Easter

death and resurrection were for nothing. They wanted a political-military leader who would give them back some civic and personal pride. Man is at his poorest when he seeks status above love. He is blindest when he seeks to dominate more than to be accepted.

What About Us?

But are we any different from the early Jews? What are we "out to get" for ourselves? Are we happy with love and acceptance, or do we long to "conquer" others: make them think we have all the answers; have a position in life to be envied by onlookers? This kind of striving medically and socially leads to ulcers and frustration.

How wonderful it would be for us to admit we're loved by a father beyond our wildest dreams. The father doesn't give two hoots about the condition of the living room sofa or the latest model car. He was happy to give us his risen son as a permanent gift. Yet we seem to be out for the wrong values. So our love of the things around us blinds us to the love of our shepherd and his father.

And in our romance with glittering things that have no heart or smile we turn around and become "hired hands" of Christ. Oh yes, we belong to the family business, but we have no love for the flock (our own brothers and sisters) and run out when it becomes difficult or demands are made on us. I'm not going to give up Monday night at the movies to attend the third grade school play. And if I do, I'm not stopping at the hospital to visit Harry's mother-in-law. Through our neglect we reject Christ the cornerstone. We proclaim that Christ is not the foundation of our values.

Peter Principle

Like Peter, if we must give an answer today to why things

BREAKING THE BREAD

are so bad in the world, it is because in practice many people have rejected the cornerstone of their lives. They refuse to follow the shepherd's lead. Money has become the main stone and public opinion (What would the bridge club think? I couldn't skip bowling. What would the boys think?) has become our leader. Yet Peter warns us: there is no salvation in anyone else, for there is no other name in the whole world given to men by which we are to be saved.

Join Now

We're totally free to follow the Lord. There's no pressure to sign up. The risen Christ turns to us and calls by name as he did for Thomas in the upper room, and Mary in the garden. He asks us to trust him during this Mass. He has our welfare at heart. The Father worries more about us than a shepherd ever would over sheep, or a boss over his workers. And Christ offers us a greater profit sharing plan than business has ever thought of. We become not only part of the Lord's work but we become one of the family. "See what love the father has bestowed on us in letting us be called children of God." If we would spend half the time thinking about and being with Christ than we do worrying about our jobs, most of our job problems would probably be eased. Make the investment and watch for results.

M. M. R.

Fifth Sunday of Easter

HOW TO TRIM YOUR PRIDE

In the late '50's all the home magazines began carrying supplements on the perfect diet. The energies of the '40's had faded away and we had become soft. Everything from grapefruit to bourbon was considered the missing element to burn away these calories. The '60's produced the cholesterol scare, canonizing the use of no-taste milk and the low cost table-spread that made you feel like a king and look like your children. And the '70's, not to be out-done, have deleted preservatives and harmful chemicals from diet food to keep us ecologically and naturally trim. And for some reason we instinctively go along with the high priests of advertising and the good advice of doctors. If you want to stay in shape, look younger and healthier, cut down on intake: life will mean much more.

It's too bad the mystics of the middle ages didn't patent their diets: fasting and self-denial. Those were the perfect combination to keep you physically sharp and spiritually in tune. And in a way this is the analogy being used by Christ: a healthy tree, bush or vine has to be pruned.

Real Problem

We merely have to translate our Lord's example and our experiences from dieting into the "realer" world of problems and disappointments. If we look on worrying and suffering as a form of trimming or dieting, slimming down our selfishness to size, we might see value in being neglected once in a while by our friends. We might see some advantage in not getting higher grades or a raise. We might profit from a current sickness, or not crab too much about arthritis. If we're not trimmed down, our pride will grow, our selfishness will expand and become bloated, but we won't grow.

Painless

Our growth doesn't have to come through pain, but we can try to distract our self-intake by being concerned about others. Listening to and remembering someone else's current problems isn't too painful and it puts us in shape. We become more "beautiful," compassionate, patient and understanding.

And the best part of this struggle is that we are not alone. We may cut back sometimes but we're still part of the vine: Christ. Branches have certain advantages: they simply have to put to use the food and strength that come from the vine.

Obligations

But we have obligations too. Christ doesn't expect miracles from us, but wants us to try with his help to reach out to others. The vine won't extend itself without the branches. And wherever the branches show up, the vine is appreciated or not according to the goodness of the branches. The Jewish Christians had a hard time deciding whether to accept Saul-Paul or not. But Paul proved he was joined to the vine by speaking out fearlessly in the name of Jesus, and worrying more about the Gospel than his own welfare.

It's not that easy staying in shape as a Christian. We have to accept pain and disappointment. We have to listen more to others than we do to ourselves. We die a little each day to make room for the Risen life. And ultimately, as Christians we look forward to the final death, the last shedding of the human bulk. But death will be a real joy: the end of sin, the end of struggling, and the new permanently trim us. If

Fifth Sunday of Easter

we try to diet our selfishness, we learn in advance what it means to die: dying to self, but rising to Christ.

Christ died to give us life—not in small proportion, but life abundantly. For this I will praise you Lord, in the assembly of your people.

M. M. R.

Sixth Sunday of Easter

OH YES, HE'S A PERSONAL FRIEND OF MINE

Have you ever had the experience of feeling talented and clever in some groups, and with others you feel you have very little to offer? Like the young father who is a champion athlete with his son around, but comes in last with his friends on the golf course. It's so much easier to share a good story with your fellow workers than it is with the supervisor. And if we look closely at this Jeckyll and Hyde situation, most of the time our "success" depends on just how much "acceptance" we enjoy from the group we're with. Without ever hearing it we know by instinct when we are appreciated and we respond. A smile or nod is like a roar of applause or hugs and kisses. We are encouraged and made confident. With this support we are good at what we're doing.

Best Friends

But strangely for all our eagerness to have a good reception, we miss our best fans: God our father and Christ our brother. "Love then consists in this: not that we have loved God, but that he has loved us." Christ knows us at our best and appreciates our efforts to try harder. How much confidence would you have if you experienced Christ as your happiest listener, your best audience? And praise the Lord, he is your best friend. Christ has laid down his life for us, made himself available at all times, and solemnly calls us friends.

Sixth Sunday of Easter

Spread the Wealth

To show our appreciation, we simply have to extend the call we've experienced to those around us. "I choose you. I call you friend." It's simply a matter of sharing the wealth. Or better, as Christ spoke to us last week, we are the branches of Christ reaching out to support those who haven't experienced the richness of the vine. This acceptance can't stop with those immediately around us. Like the proverbial pebble in the brook the circle has to widen if Christianity is to keep its slogan: look how they love one another. Peter had to be told by the Holy Spirit to open the circle of the Church wider to take in Cornelius.

And how much sooner might there be a unity of churches if we Catholics were simply to convince other Christians of our acceptance of them. No suspicions, no better-than-thou notions would be the way to start. We would still be painfully aware of differences in doctrines. But we easily allow our friends to have different opinions and continue fully to accept them. Why not treat other Christian assemblies the same way?

Easter Example

Christ has certainly set the pace. The Easter joy of the apostles was based on the risen Lord's re-establishing the bond of friendship. After all, the apostles had run out on Christ during the crucifixion. But peace-be-with-you wiped away fear and guilt and their joy was made complete.

If you don't think you have much skill in bringing Christians together, try short steps. Watch for occasions just to compliment those around you at work or school. This mild acceptance they experience will make them more responsive

BREAKING THE BREAD

to your friendship. Your love will grow and the Lord will make you bolder to share deeper values about your God and your church.

Within this Mass there are friends around you ready to support you, to wish you peace. And don't forget. You have a very influential friend upstairs. He'll back you up all the way.

M. M. R.

Solemnity of the Ascension
Suggested Use: First Eucharistic
Prayer with Special Communicantes

THE FLOWER OF THE RESURRECTION

The Ascension tends to be neglected among the great mysteries of the life of Jesus Christ. We commemorate the birth of Jesus in the joy of Christmas. We appreciate the magnitude of his death as the sacrifice of the cross. We celebrate his resurrection in the glory of Easter. But the Ascension? It is tucked away in the quiet of a middle-of-the-week observance, almost as if we are not quite sure what to do with it.

Integral Part

We can understand the place of the Ascension only if we see it in relationship to the other central events in the life of Jesus. Jesus was born as one of us so that he could enter into the human situation as our Savior. He came to rescue us from our twin enemies, sin and eternal death. By his sacrificial death Jesus won the victory over sin and death, and that victory was manifested in his resurrection. Jesus made the passage through the darkness of death and emerged triumphant in the light of his resurrection. But Jesus did not rise merely to take up again the earthly existence that he had begun at the moment of his incarnation. The ascension shows that he rose from the dead to a new, heavenly life. His ascension was his return to the Father, his glorification in heaven at God's right hand, his exaltation as the Lord of Life. The ascension is an integral part of the resurrection itself, as the fruit is part of the tree, or better, as a full-blown flower is the purpose of stem and bud. The ascension indicates the newness and fullness of the risen life of Jesus Christrist. We really cannot imagine what this life is like. In fact we don't even have a good word to describe it, but there is one word you will hear repeated in the Mass, an inadequate word, the only word we have, and that word is glory. Jesus ascended to a life of glory.

Our Life

The ascension of Jesus is important to us because life is precious. We cling to life in this world, despite all the sorrow, all the pain, all the frustration of human existence. We cling to this life because it is the only life we know. And yet we really do not want this kind of life forever. We yearn for the perfect life that will never end, the life of glory.

In times past men searched for the fountain of youth so that they might always be young and never have to die. Their searching strikes us today as a little naïve. But some scientists today are almost as naïve as they probe into the aging process in the hope of finding a way to prolong life and eventually prevent death itself. Such searching and probing miss the point. The life we are made for is not found in this world, but in heaven, and to find it we must, like Christ, pass through death to a sharing in his resurrection and ascension.

Hope

We have been called to a great hope in Christ. In him our frail human nature has been raised to glory. One day his glorious heritage will be ours. We do not have to fear a physical aging process that will lead to death; we need fear only the disruptive power of sin which alone can destroy us. Jesus has given us the victory over sin. Today as we look toward heaven, toward Jesus in glory at the right hand of the Father, we do so with the belief that he will come again to raise us to a sharing in the fullness of life, the life of glory.

C. E. M.

Seventh Sunday of Easter

JUMP, I'LL CATCH YOU

It's amazing how the problem of faith is so similar for people at any age. College students, housewives all speak the same: "If I could only see and experience Jesus as the apostles or as the saints did, then I could easily believe."

And just as amazing, the problem seems to have been the same for the apostles: if only they could see God the Father, then they could believe. "Lord, when will you show us the Father?" Our Lord opens his arms and simply asks them to make the jump of faith: when you see me, you see the Father. And evidently they jumped.

Our Faith

This means that our faith begins with faith in the testimony of those who first believed in Christ. We accept their impression, their convictions that Jesus is Lord, Christ is God. We place our natural trust first in their faith, their acceptance of Christ. Then our accepting this "second hand" faith, thanks to wonderful grace, becomes first hand faith and even leads to the real experience of Christ.

We are Chosen

But we shouldn't think this two-step process puts Christ at a distance from us. Our faith is a response to a personal call. The choice of Matthias in the first reading is one of the most un-celebrated yet significant steps in the early Church. Matthias is the second generation of believers along

Seventh Sunday of Easter

with Titus, Timothy, Barsabbas, Barnabas and us. Christ choosing Matthias through the other apostles is as good as Christ choosing us through the Church today. "You have not chosen me, I have chosen you."

Love to See

We have been hand picked just to experience God. And John describes this process of discovering God. No one has ever seen God. Right. Even Moses on Mt. Sinai had his face shielded from the vision of God. But John tells us that God is love. And any of the chosen who abide in love, abide in God already. Second step: any of the chosen who acknowledge that Jesus is the son of God, God dwells in him and he in God.

The World

The Father is with us, ready to be experienced, if we can only wake up. If only we can dislodge ourselves from our "world" of hurry-up, quadrasonic purple frozen foods, new cars and new duds, we will be free to see. If we recognize that we don't belong to radios and TV's, we're not cousins of the freeways, we're not owned by the world—then the joy of Christ can be made complete in us. Faith helps us recognize that our father is God, our brother is Christ and our name is Christian, not "Worldling."

All in the Family

And Christ has worked hard to keep us together. He reminds us of his death for us through the marks in his hands and feet. He has transcended all limitations through his resur-

BREAKING THE BREAD

rection to be with us this morning at Mass. He is here to literally protect and guard us from our goofy world. The Risen Lord reminds us we have been chosen to succeed the apostles; to spread the presence of God through our love for each other; and to realize we don't need to depend on things that rust for complete joy.

Maybe we spend too much time and energy reaching out for the Lord. Too bad. He is right next to us and we're too exhausted to experience him and too afraid to make a tiny jump.

M. M. R.

Pentecost Sunday

THE GIFT OF WISDOM

It is not difficult to imagine the condition of the apostles after Jesus had ascended to heaven. They felt alone and scared, like so many little children lost in a big city among unfriendly people. They huddled together in the upper room, confused and frightened, not knowing what to do or where to turn, or what was to become of them. They had indeed heard Jesus proclaim that he would not leave them alone, that he would send the Holy Spirit, but the meaning of his promise had not penetrated their befuddled minds.

Coming of the Spirit

Then on the day of Pentecost Jesus fulfilled his promise. In a marvelous manifestation he sent the Holy Spirit to his apostles. They were changed in an instant. They went forth before the crowds gathered for the feast of Pentecost and preached Christ with boldness and almost careless abandon. And remember that these were the same men who had run away in fear when Jesus was arrested. Among them was Peter, who during the passion had been afraid to admit to a young servant girl that he even knew Jesus.

Courage

Obviously Peter and the other apostles enjoyed a new-found courage. The change within them, however, was more fundamental than a transformation of cowardice into bravery. They now experienced a completely different outlook on life. They no longer felt alone and confused. They knew what was really important: not whether they were safe or not, or even whether they lived or died; what was really important was that they be on Christ's side and do his will. In an instant it was perfectly clear to them that Jesus really mattered. They had a new, incisive sense of values. In a word, they had received the gift of wisdom.

Wisdom

The gift of wisdom which transformed the apostles is a gift that we possess too. We experienced our own personal Pentecost when we were confirmed. There was no marvelous manifestation, only the simple sacramental ceremony. But in the sacrament of confirmation Jesus truly sent his Holy Spirit to us with all his gifts, including the gift of wisdom. Why is it then that we are often confused and befuddled? Why are we seemingly so different from the transformed apostles? One reason is that we sometimes put obstacles in the way of our wisdom. We let our sense of values get mixed up.

It is not surprising that we become confused about real values. It is very likely that we find this day of Pentecost a time for paying bills without money, a time for trying to make ends meet when the ends seem miles apart. We are pressured by advertising which attempts to create a feeling of need within us for unnecessary items, and which tries to stimulate desires for the bigger and the better. We live in a society wherein the yardstick of success is financial gain, a criterion which induces tensions and anxieties.

False Pressures

Even children become victims of false pressures. A young boy must be a star on the little league baseball team, and to strike out with the bases loaded becomes a tragedy both for him and his parents. A little girl must be cute and attrac-

Pentecost Sunday

tive and wear the latest little girl styles, or she is a failure in her own eyes and a disappointment to her father and mother. Teenagers sense the pressures to be popular, to go along with what is the "in" thing, not to be a drag or a prude. Some college students feel impelled to get a degree, no matter what may be the value of the courses they are taking, while others judge that their college careers are irrelevant if they are not involved in some protest movement.

Something Fundamental

It is not surprising that we find ourselves so different from the apostles on the day of Pentecost. This feast of Pentecost has always been looked upon as a celebration to stimulate our apostolic spirit so that we may live the Christian life with courage and proclaim the truth of Christ with boldness both by words and actions. But there is something more fundamental than courage and boldness, and that something is the gift of wisdom. That wisdom we all desperately need.

A New Opportunity

Today on this feast of Pentecost we have the opportunity to renew our gift of wisdom, our sense of values. In this Mass we should pray that we may see what is really important, not whether we are rich or popular or whatever, but whether we are on Christ's side, whether we are really trying to live according to the teachings of Jesus. We should pray that we may be able to see clearly what is really important in life. The gift of wisdom is indeed a great gift from God because it can give us a true sense of values.

C. E. M.

Trinity Sunday

IT'S ALL VERY PERSONAL

It is a great sign of friendship to tell someone a secret about yourself. You simply do not tell your secrets to enemies. And the more personal and intimate the secret, the more personal and intimate is the friendship. In fact, you tell the secret not only as a sign of friendship but also as a way of getting closer to your friend, for your secret is part of yourself.

Revelation

Jesus has a great love of friendship for us. It is not surprising, then, that he has revealed secrets to us about himself. Because his love is so personal and intimate, the secrets are personal and intimate. Jesus saved the most personal and intimate secret of all until the night before he died. It was not until the time of the Last Supper that Jesus fully revealed to us, in the persons of the apostles, the great mystery of the Trinity.

The mystery of the Trinity is the secret concerning the inmost private life of God. The Jews, chosen people though they were, did not know that there are three persons in God. As we read in the first lesson, God revealed himself to Moses as "Lord," the one great God, creator and master of the whole world. We are privileged through Jesus to know about the great truth of the Trinity.

Our Belief

Because of the revelation of Jesus we as Catholics believe that in the one God there are three persons. The first person is the Father. He is called Father because he is the source of life for the Son. The second person is called Son because he receives his life from the Father. Father and Son love each other with a love more complete and perfect than we can imagine. Their love is so perfect that it is a person, the Holy Spirit. This third person, as the personal love between Father and Son, is the bond of union or oneness between Father and Son.

Mystery

The Trinity is indeed a great mystery, one we will never fully understand. Mysterious though it is, the Trinity should mean very much to us. Maybe we too often think of God as just God, some indefinite, nebulous blur in our minds, not as three real persons. Even when we pray, perhaps we do so with a word on our lips, such as "God" or "Jesus," but without any deep realization that prayer is a very personal matter. You see, God has called us to enter into a personal relationship with himself and the relationship that we have to each person is different.

Our Relationships

We are the children of God the Father, and we must think of him as a Father when we pray to him. We are his children because we have become like the second person, his Son. Never of course can we be equal to the Son, but we do stand in somewhat the same relationship as he does to the Father. The Holy Spirit has been given us to make us sons of the Father. He is the bond of union that makes us one with God the Son.

BREAKING THE BREAD

Liturgy

Without a realization of our relationship to the three persons we may find the liturgical way of praying a bit strange. Notice that almost all the prayers of the Mass are spoken to God the Father. Those prayers are addressed to the Father through, with, and in the Son. They are done so in union with the Holy Spirit. We find this attitude of prayer all through the Mass but there is one classic example. That example is called the great doxology, and it comes at the conclusion of the Eucharistic Prayer. The priest holding up the body and blood of Jesus, the Son, looks to heaven and says to God the Father: "Through him, with him, in him, in the unity of the Holy Spirit all glory and honor is yours, almighty Father, for ever and ever." That magnificent prayer reflects our relationships with the three persons. Our prayer of praise is directed to the Father because everything, even life itself, comes from him. We pray through, with, and in Jesus because we share in his sonship. We pray in the unity of the Holy Spirit because he unites us to the Son.

The Christian Outlook

All this is not to say that we must not pray to God the Son or to the Holy Spirit. We should. In fact before we can pray in the liturgical way we must develop a real devotion to both God the Son and the Holy Spirit. But we must come to appreciate the value of praying to the Father through the Son in the Holy Spirit. After all, when Jesus taught us to pray he said, "When you pray, say 'Our Father.'" It has been observed that Christianity is not so much looking at Jesus as it is looking in the same direction as he, that is, to the Father. We stand in somewhat the same relationship that

Jesus does as son of the Father. And it is the Holy Spirit who gives us that relationship.

Very Personal

And so the Trinity is indeed a very important mystery for us, not just something to believe and then forget all about. This great truth should shape our attitude toward the three persons of God and influence our prayer. Indeed the mystery of the Trinity is a very personal matter.

C. E. M.

Solemnity of Corpus Christi
(Sunday after Trinity Sunday)

Suggested acclamation: "When we eat this bread and drink this cup, we proclaim your death, Lord Jesus, until you come in glory."

"I NEED A CROSS"

Once many years ago there was a young boy who, after his daily chores were done, would love to sit and rest beneath a certain tree. He would eat of her apples and doze in the shade of her branches. The tree was happy that the boy enjoyed her so much. But the time came when the boy grew up and went away to another part of the country, and that made the tree very sad indeed. About a year later the boy returned, but he was followed by a large crowd and the tree was afraid that the boy would not even notice her with all the people around him. The tree was not sure, but she thought the boy gave her a special look as he passed by, though he obviously had no time to stop.

Then one day the boy came back all alone. The tree was overjoyed for she thought that now the boy would once more eat her apples and doze in the shade of her branches. The tree noticed, however, that the boy seemed troubled. "Tree," said the boy, "you have always been good to me. Now I am in very great need of a cross, but I have no wood to make one." The tree replied eagerly, "Come, cut me down to a stump and with my wood you can make a beautiful cross." The boy did so, and as he walked away carrying the wood on his shoulders the tree was very happy to have done this great favor for the boy.

While she was still thinking of how much she loved the boy, the tree, now only a stump, looked up to a hill and

Solemnity of Corpus Christi

there she saw her boy dead upon the cross made from the wood. The poor stump cried and said, "I do not understand. Why did this boy have to die? And on a cross made from my wood?" All that night and through the next day and the following night, everything was dark. All the other trees and bushes and flowers seemed to shrink within themselves. But on the third morning the sun came out bright and strong and all the birds started to sing. Everything seemed alive and happy again. The stump woke up and she saw standing there before her, looking all radiant in light, her boy whom she loved so much. He was smiling at her so happily that the stump felt a little embarrassed and she lowered her eyes. When she did so, she saw that she was no longer a mere stump. Her trunk and all her branches had suddenly grown back and she was more beautiful than ever before.*

The Cross

It is hard for us to understand why Jesus had to die on a cross. In the plan of God it was somehow necessary that he die for us to restore us to the love of the Father. Jesus loved life. It was not easy for him to die. And yet in obedience to his Father he was willing to open his arms on the cross to include us in his embrace of love. Death, however, was not the end of God's plan, only the beginning, for Jesus went through death to life, to the eternal life of the resurrection.

For hundreds of years the sacrifices prescribed through Moses, of which we were reminded in today's first reading, were duly offered, but they could not get the job done. In the second reading we were told what happened through the cross: "When Christ came as high priest of the good things which came to be, he entered once for all into the sanctuary . . . not with the blood of goats and calves but with

---

* Suggested by *The Giving Tree*, a book by Shel Silverstein, published by Harper and Row.

his own blood, and achieved eternal redemption." Jesus went before us in death so that we could follow him to resurrection.

The Mass

We can share in the resurrection of Christ only if we are willing to share in his death as well. Though Jesus died once and cannot die again, through the Mass he gives us an opportunity, an invitation, to share in the offering of his sacrificial death. "At the Last Supper, on the night when he was betrayed, our Savior instituted the eucharistic sacrifice of his body and blood. He did this in order to perpetuate the sacrifice of the cross throughout the centuries until he should come again" (Constitution on the Liturgy, 47). Here in the Mass Jesus does not want to be alone as he perpetuates his sacrifice. He says to you, "I am in very great need of a cross but have no wood to make one." He hopes you will reply eagerly, "Come, cut me down to a stump and with my wood you can make a beautiful cross." Jesus wants you. He wants you to become part of his sacrifice, to offer yourself with him.

In the eucharistic acclamation we will say: "When we eat this bread and drink this cup, we proclaim your death, Lord Jesus, until you come in glory." "To proclaim his death" means more than the having of words on our lips. We must become dead with Christ—dead to our sins, to our selfishness, to our lack of love. Are you willing to cut yourself down to a stump for the sake of Christ? Do you love Christ enough to die physically for him? Make the decision. Give yourself. Then one day through the darkness of death you will see Christ standing before you, looking all radiant in light, and smiling at you. And you will see that you are no longer a stump, that you have grown to the beautiful fullness of eternal life.

C. E. M.   O. J. M.

Note: The Tenth, Eleventh, and Twelfth Sundays of the Year do not appear in the B cycle for 1973 or 1976. Only the Twelfth Sunday will be used in 1979. Brief homilies for these Sundays are included, however, in the event that their readings are chosen at some time in accord with paragraph 332 of the General Instruction on the Roman Missal.

Tenth Sunday of the Year

A Household Divided

The first reading today is typically human. Adam and Eve are much like two children, neither of whom is willing to accept responsibility for having done wrong. The scene is similar to that in which a father comes home to find the television set broken. He says to his young son, "Didn't I tell you not to fool around with the television?" The boy replies, pointing to his little sister, "Don't blame me; she made me turn it on." And the little girl explains, "My friend came over and wanted to watch TV."

Dissension and Division

Adam, like the little boy, refused to accept responsibility and blamed the woman. More seriously he even implied that God was somewhat at fault as he said, "The woman whom *you* put here with me—she gave me fruit from the tree." The woman in her turn also implicitly involved God as she blamed the serpent, for the serpent was likewise a creature of God. Dissension and division were the result of sin, but they were also its occasion. If Adam and his wife had stuck together, unified by their loyalty to God, they could have overcome the temptation to evil. The words of Jesus in the gospel, though spoken of the forces of evil, apply equally to mankind: "If a household is divided according to its loyalties, that household will not survive."

Enmity

We simply cannot afford dissension and division among ourselves since we are engaged in a bitter war against evil. God proclaimed, speaking to the serpent as the symbol of the forces of evil, "I will put enmity between you and the woman, between your offspring and hers." Enmity means all-out conflict to the end with no truce, no compromise, until one force emerges as the victor. Jesus through his cross and resurrection has won the victory in himself. If we are going to share in that victory, we have to stick together, united through our unswerving loyalty to him.

Unity and Peace

In the Eucharistic Prayer we beg God to grant us unity. That must not be an idle prayer. Together we receive Jesus in holy communion as our bond of union with each other. That reception of the Body of Christ must not be an empty ritual. Before communion we are urged to exchange a sign of peace, but true peace can come only through our victory over sin and evil. Our sign of peace, then, can be offered with sincerity and effectiveness only if we come forward to receive Jesus with eagerness to share his love with everyone without exception, for only the union of Christian love can lead us to victory over sin and evil.

Our enmity with the forces of evil will last until Christ comes again in glory. If we as the brothers and sisters of Christ, as the household of God, remain united in our loyalty to our heavenly Father we can have the firm confidence of sharing in Christ's final victory.

C. E. M.

Eleventh Sunday of the Year*

A GROWING ORGANISM

No one has actually seen a tree grow. Its growth is too slow for the human eye to perceive. Nor for that matter has anyone ever seen a child grow. It is only after you have not been with a child for some time that you notice how tall he has become. Living things grow slowly.

The Church

The Church too grows slowly because it is a living organism. It is made up of human beings who, like the cells of the human body, form the mystical body of Jesus Christ. Growth is what our Lord is talking about in today's gospel. He started with the twelve apostles, a very small group of men. Those men after Pentecost went out and began the conversion of the whole world so that today the Church has more than half a billion people as its members. About one in every six persons is a Catholic. When Pope John summoned the Second Vatican Council more than two thousand bishops from every nation responded to his call. If the apostles could come back to earth today, they would be amazed at the growth of the Church.

God's Part

The growth of the Church is of course due to the power of God, and God's power cannot be frustrated by either the evil or the incompetence of men. As a seed planted in the earth has an almost mysterious ability to develop while the farmer sleeps, so the Church has an inner divinely given

* This Sunday will not appear in the B cycle until after 1979.

dynamism which insures its continuing and spreading from age to age. And yet the role of the members of the Church is far from passive in God's plan. What God could do all by himself he has decided to do with and through the members of the Church.

Pius XII

Back in 1943 when he wrote his encyclical on the Church as the Mystical Body of Christ, Pope Pius XII put it this way: "Dying on the cross Christ left to his Church the immense treasury of the redemption; towards this she contributed nothing. But when those graces come to be distributed, not only does he share this task of sanctification with his Church, but he wants it in a way to be due to her action" (46). That you and I are Catholics today is traceable to the action of those who have preceded us in the faith. That the Church spread from Palestine over the centuries to all the countries of the world is due, under God, to the goodness and holiness of the members of the Church.

When we think of how the Church began with such a small group and see what it is today we are indeed amazed, but we must never become complacent. We should wish that everyone without exception might be a full, complete member of the Church. Now it is our turn to do something, for we bear the responsibility for continuing the spread of Christ's Church. We know that we should give good example and try to talk to people about the Church. Today, however, let's try to focus on something very important, something that may escape our realization.

The Body of Christ

The Church is like a human body. As the vitality of the body depends on the health of its cells, so the vitality of the Church depends on the holiness of its members. We may think that the sins we commit offend God alone and harm only ourselves. That is not true. Sin damages the whole Church, just as an infection in any part of the body affects the whole body. On the other hand, we may feel that we are not very important, that our prayers and penances cannot accomplish very much. That too is not true. When we try to live good lives as Jesus has taught us we are very instrumental in the building up of the whole Church.

Deep Mystery

Listen to these words of Pope Pius XII from the same encyclical on The Mystical Body: "Deep mystery this, subject of inexhaustible meditation, that the salvation of many depends on the prayers and voluntary penances which the members of the Mystical Body of Jesus Christ offer for this intention..." (*ibid.*). Deep mystery indeed: God wills that the salvation of others should come about through our prayers and penances. Subject of inexhaustible meditation, something we must never forget, that the goodness of our lives can really benefit others.

C. E. M.

Twelfth Sunday of the Year*

STORMS AND TRUST

One evening, after preaching to the people all day long, Jesus asked his disciples to take him by boat across the Sea of Galilee. Jesus was worn out from his labors and was apparently looking for a little rest and relaxation. He was so exhausted in fact that he fell asleep in the stern even as strong winds began to buffet the light fishing craft. Sudden squalls on the Sea of Galilee are not extraordinary. The Sea, about 685 feet below sea level, is surrounded by mountains on almost all sides. As the warm air rises in the evening, cool air rushes down from the mountains and in a short time can transform the calm water into dangerous waves of seven or eight feet. Jesus was sleeping serenely during just such a violent disturbance. In panic the disciples woke Jesus with pleas for help.

Rebuke

Jesus then did exactly what we would expect him to do. He rebuked the wind and said to the sea, "Quiet! Be still!" Immediately there came a great calm. Then Jesus did something unexpected. He rebuked the disciples just as he had rebuked the wind. In effect he said to them as he did to the sea, "Quiet! Be still!" Jesus appeared annoyed that they had become terrified, but who wouldn't be terrified in such a situation? What had the disciples done wrong? In a time of crisis they turned to Jesus for much needed help—it seemed the only thing to do. And yet Jesus complained, "Why are you lacking in faith?"

* This Sunday will not appear in the B cycle until 1979.

Twelfth Sunday of the Year

Faith Lacking

Jesus' point was that the disciples should have had more confidence in him. Jesus knew what he was doing when he told them to cross the Sea. He put them into the dangerous situation and they should have had complete trust that he would take care of them. It was only after they had exhausted all human means to save themselves as they bailed water and adjusted the rudder to bring the ship to, that they *finally* thought to wake Jesus. In other words, they looked to Jesus for help only as a last resort when all else had failed, whereas, though still using human means, their very first thought should have been of Jesus. They had not yet come to the realization that Jesus, whom they called "Teacher," was actually the Lord and Master of all creation (cf. first reading).

Trust Needed

What about our faith and trust in God? Imagine this scene which takes place somewhere every day. A person surrounded by his family lies dying in a hospital bed. The doctors have admitted that the case is medically hopeless. A member of the family, out of the hearing of the sick man, murmurs, "I guess all we can do now is pray." All we can do now is pray . . . . Such a statement betrays a lack of real faith, an attitude that turning to God in prayer is but a last resort in dire circumstances. It resembles that lack of trust found in the disciples during the storm on the Sea. Jesus wishes to teach us today that our attitude must be different, that our prayer of trust as we turn to God for help must be an habitual part of our life in all its circumstances. We must use human means to help ourselves, but not with the idea that we will turn to God only after all our own efforts have failed.

Prayer

God should not be the last person we think of as we are buffeted by the storms of life. We should not wait until the violent winds blow before we pray to God. A little child does not turn to his parents only when he is in serious trouble. He is completely dependent on them and somehow feels that all good things come from them. He looks to his parents for food when he is hungry, he runs to them for comfort when he has skinned his knee or had his feelings hurt, he seeks solace from them when he is lonely and blue. Above all he wants to feel that he belongs, that he has their love and interest all the time.

No matter how young or old we may be, in relation to God we are like little children, and God is a Father more loving and interested than even the best of human parents. He wants us to look to him in all the circumstances of our lives, not merely when we are in serious trouble. God is Lord and Master not only of the universe but of our individual lives as well. He has placed us in this world, he knew what he was doing, and he will take care of us if we have real faith and trust in him.

All Circumstances

The prayer of trust, then, is not some last ditch effort to ward off impending disaster as suggested in the words heard so often, "All we can do now is pray." It should instead be a child's confident turning to God as a loving Father. In all the circumstances of our lives, we should pray with confidence in the words our Savior gave us: "Our Father."

C. E. M.

Thirteenth Sunday of the Year

GOD HAS TIME FOR PEOPLE

What is God really like? Did he create the world and then send it spinning into space with little concern, or is he still interested in the welfare of his creatures? Is he so busy looking after the big, important people of the world who shape history itself that he has no time to look after all the little people like you and me? Is he patient with our foibles, tolerant of our failures, understanding toward our pettiness? What indeed is God really like? Actually we can come to know what God the Father is like by coming to know Jesus, his Son, as he is set forth in the pages of the gospels.

Two Facts

There are two facts about Jesus which we must constantly keep balanced in our minds. The first is that he is truly divine, the Son of God, the perfect image of his Father. The second is that he is truly human, just as human as we are in everything except sin. Since Jesus is truly God, the image of his Father, we can know what God is like by knowing Jesus. Since Jesus is truly human, through him we can get to know God in a human way. In other words, Jesus reveals God to us through his humanity. As Jesus said to Philip the Apostle at the Last Supper, "Whoever has seen me has seen the Father" (Jn 14:9).

Revelation

Today's gospel contains an important revelation about God as seen through the humanity of Jesus.* As the narrative

---

* The Introduction to the Gospel according to Mark as found in

133

BREAKING THE BREAD

begins a large crowd had gathered around Jesus. It was an excellent opportunity for him to communicate his message to a considerable number of people. Like a good teacher Jesus no doubt had a "lesson plan," a well-thought-out instruction he wished to impart that day. He had scarcely begun when Jairus, one of the officials of the synagogue, interrupted him with an earnest appeal for his critically ill daughter. Seeing the distress of the father Jesus was willing to abandon his own plans in order to meet the needs of the man kneeling before him, and prepared to follow him home. Though he uttered no word of complaint, Jesus must have been wondering where the man lived, how long it would take to get to his home and return, and whether all his potential hearers would still be waiting for him when he got back.

At that moment, with all these thoughts running through his mind, Jesus felt someone touch him, the woman with the hemorrhage. It would have been very understandable if Jesus had become impatient, if he had said something like, "Woman, don't bother me now. Can't you see that this important man wants me to save his daughter from death? You and your problem can wait!" Instead, Jesus realized that this poor woman was important too, and that her problem, though not nearly as great as that of Jairus, was big to her. With compassion in his eyes and sympathy in his voice, he said gently, "Daughter, it is your faith that has cured you. Go in peace and be free of this illness." But before he could finish

---

the St. Joseph Edition of the NAB points out: "Although the gospel of Mark is developed in connection with the Christian faith in Jesus as redeemer and Son of God, its contents indicate the historical reality of the person and ministry of Jesus in a manner less refined by theological reflection than the accounts of the other evangelists. In Mark the person of Jesus is depicted with an unaffected naturalness. He reacts to events with authentic human emotions." Bruce Vawter, C.M. in *The Four Gospels* (p. 167) observes that the details of this pericope suggest accurate historical recollection rather than dramatic invention.

Thirteenth Sunday of the Year

speaking with the woman, he was interrupted again by the friends of the official who arrived to say that the girl was dead. Undaunted by this information, Jesus turned his attention back to Jairus, followed him home, and raised the girl to life.

Time for People

Let me tell you what this gospel says to me about God. It says that God is not too busy running the universe, that he really does have time for people, big people like Jairus and little people like the unnamed woman. When I talk to God about my difficulties, I am not afraid that he will reply, "I would really like to help you, but I just don't have time; I am too busy looking after important people like the Pope and the President." This gospel says that God understands human nature and realizes that my problems are very relative— relative to me! I think we have all been struck by the statement of the man who said, "I complained because I had no shoes until I met a man who had no feet." Though that encounter helped to put poverty in perspective, it did not really solve the man's problem for it failed to put shoes on his feet, and that is what he needed. My problems, though perhaps small in comparison with those of others, are big to me simply because they are my problems. God recognizes this fact. I am confident that he will never turn away from my prayers for help and protest, "Look, I have bigger things to worry about."

Finally this gospel says that God finds no problem too little to bother with or too big to solve, not a non-fatal hemorrhage nor death itself. My faith is that God will see me through *all* the difficulties of this life and will finally lead me successfully through death to eternal life.

I for one am very grateful that the events described in

BREAKING THE BREAD

today's gospel were so vividly remembered by the early Christians and recorded with such detail by the evangelist, for this gospel tells me that God does indeed have time for people. God has time for you and me.

C. E M.

Fourteenth Sunday of the Year

A PROPHET WITHOUT HONOR?

One of the most common failures of our human condition is that we tend to take things and people for granted, especially if they have become very familiar to us. A college professor once observed that students soon become bored with their regular instructors and fail to appreciate their scholarship. They either doze through their classes or skip them altogether, but flock with eagerness to hear the special lecture of an "expert." The expert need not be better informed or more astute than the members of the faculty. His appealing mark of distinction is that he is different—from another college or university, with a beard, a foreign accent, and preferably a slight limp.

Home Town Prophet

One time when Jesus returned to his home town of Nazareth, he stood up to preach on the sabbath in the synagogue. He met with opposition because he failed to manifest any mark of distinction. The people did not complain that his message was shallow or inane. Actually they were openly amazed at what he had to say. Their objection was based on the fact that he was too familiar to them. They could not accept this home town boy turned prophet. They knew him as the village carpenter, the son of Mary, a woman they had seen coming and going like all the other women of the area. And now they heard Jesus speaking in their local synagogue with the Galilean accent which was characteristic of their own speech. Jesus perceived their negative reaction

BREAKING THE BREAD

and summed it up by saying, "No prophet is without honor except in his native place, among his own kindred, and in his own house."

The Familiar

Is Jesus without honor, or at least proper honor, here in his own house, this church? We have heard the gospel so many times, we have become so familiar with the discourses, parables, and miracles of Jesus that we run the risk of failing to appreciate it all because it has become too familiar to us. Sometimes we may even put more faith in the words of some magazine author or commentator on television than we do in the words of Jesus Christ.

There is a real danger that we may take the entire Mass for granted. Even though the Mass in recent years has undergone a marvelous restoration through changes suggested by the profound scholarship of liturgical experts and introduced by the supreme authority of the Church, the "new" Mass is already becoming "old" and familiar to us. Actually the Mass should be a wonderful experience for us, but in order to make it such we need more than all the externals of celebration which may now surround it. We need individual, personal reflection. Let me offer a few suggestions, which I hope you will think about very carefully.

Reflection

As you drive or walk to church, or in the few moments you may have before Mass begins, make the effort to impress on yourself what is about to happen. Say to yourself: "God is about to speak to me in the scriptures, and I will reply to God in the prayers and hymns. Jesus will make the great sacrifice of the cross truly present on the altar and

Fourteenth Sunday of the Year

he will give me the opportunity, with my fellow Catholics, to join with him in this offering to our Father. Then I will receive Jesus in holy communion as a pledge of my own resurrection as well as a means of strength to carry on until the day when he comes again." It will take you even less time to make this reflection than it takes me to say it now.

Then during communion or when the Mass is over, spend a moment or two in thinking about what has happened, trying to realize that you must strive to live a life in accord with the teaching you have heard and in fulfillment of the offering you have made of yourself to God.

Problems

Of course there are problems with my suggestions. You may be thinking that it is easy for me as a priest to do all these things because I live next door to the church and can get here in a matter of seconds and because I don't have to get a whole family ready to come to Mass. That's all true. My point is that if you want to appreciate the Mass you have to make an extra effort to do so. If you find you are always late for the 10:45 Mass, pretend that the Mass begins at 10:30. That will give you an extra fifteen minutes for the unexpected. While driving to Church, instead of discussing what you are going to do *after* Mass, try to talk about what you are going to do *during* Mass. When you get to church a few moments early, having benefited from the extra fifteen minutes you allowed, you parents could remind the kids to settle back and think about the Mass—which can serve as a reminder to yourselves. And rather than being the first ones out of church, take just a little time to think about what has happened and how you should try to live through the day and the week coming up. And it would be a great idea to talk about that on the way home in the car.

BREAKING THE BREAD

The Mass, however simple and familiar it may be, is just too important to take for granted. Jesus and his Mass should not be without honor either here in his house, the church, or in our minds and hearts.

C. E. M.

Fifteenth Sunday of the Year

CHANGE AND PERMANENCE

Within the past thirty years or so more profound changes have occurred than in all of previous recorded history. These changes have affected people's way of living, moral and social values, education, communications—virtually every phase of human existence. Even our language changes radically because of the constant introduction of new words as well as a new meaning given to old words. If William Shakespeare were to come to the United States today he would be able to understand only five out of every nine words in our vocabulary. The greatest writer of the English language would be semi-illiterate. As one author has put it, we have witnessed the death of permanence.*

Symbolic

Almost symbolic of the death of permanence is the frequency with which Americans move from place to place. In each year since 1948, one out of every five Americans changed his address. In one year alone, between March 1967 and March 1968, over thirty-six million citizens took up new residences, many of them in cities far removed from their previous home. Moving means, of course, the loss of old friends and familiar scenes, the need to find new schools for the children as well as another doctor and dentist, and so on in an almost infinite list of necessities. Coupled with the profundity of change is the extreme rapidity with which

---

* Alvin Toffler in his book, *Future Shock*, published by Random House. All statistics in this homily are taken from this book.

BREAKING THE BREAD

change takes place, especially in the field of knowledge. On the very day he graduates from college, a young person's education is already out-of-date. The speed of change is so great that nothing in our society seems stable or reliable. This modern phenomenon takes its toll on all but the young. The constant need to adjust and keep up with the times taxes the mind as well as the body, with the result that many people live in an unrelenting state of anxiety and confusion.

Changes in the Church

Perhaps without realizing it we look for something that has not changed, something familiar and comforting. For many of us that means our faith, our religion. One thing we always used to hear about the Catholic Church was that it could not change. Well, if you have that idea in your head—keep it there! It is true. And yet in the Church too we have seen a lot of changes in recent times, in the Mass for example, and even in some of our practices, such as Friday abstinence. How can the supposedly unchangeable Church be changing so much? The explanation lies in the fact that the Church remains the same in essentials and changes only in incidentals. Though some people easily confuse incidentals with essentials, we can readily see that there is a real difference between them. We ourselves throughout life remain the same essentially and change incidentally. When we were conceived in our mother's womb, we were only a tiny, single cell. That cell began to divide and multiply, and then one day we were born. We began to grow and to develop so that today we are very different from what we were the day we were born, and vastly different from what we were at the moment of our conception. Through all these incidental, though rather significant changes, we each remain the same

Fifteenth Sunday of the Year

person. There is something about a person which makes him who he is, and it is that essential something which cannot change.

Still the Same

The same is true of the Church. It changes in incidentals and remains the same in essentials. For instance, in today's gospel we saw Jesus send the apostles out to preach the need for repentance. Today the Church still preaches that need for repentance. Repentance means a turning away from sin and turning toward God. The Church no longer commands Friday abstinence as an expression of repentance because the form is incidental. Rather she encourages greater charity and prayer as a form of repentance because that seems better suited to our times and needs.

The Church continues to proclaim the essential message we heard in today's second reading. God the Father has chosen us to become his children, freed from sin by the blood of Jesus Christ and sealed by the power of the Holy Spirit who is our bond of union with the Father and each other. As the family of God we are called to praise and thank God by means of the Eucharistic Sacrifice for all his wonderful goodness towards us. That sacrifice was first offered by Jesus himself at the Last Supper in Aramaic. Then it was offered in Greek, later in Latin and other languages. Today we offer the very same sacrifice in English. The language of the Mass is incidental. It is what *happens* at Mass that is essential, and that has remained the same down through the centuries.

An Old Home

In a sense the Church is like an old home in which a family has lived for generations. One day the head of the family decides that the old home needs a little updating. He begins to paint the whole house, put in electricity and install modern plumbing. During the renovation the family continues to live in the home, and it proves to be a trying time. Everybody is disturbed by the inconvenience and some think it was all a big mistake. It would have been better, they feel, to have left the old house the way it was or even to have abandoned it and moved to a new place. Then one day the renovation is complete. Only then is every member of the family convinced that the father had the right idea, that all the inconvenience was more than worth it. The Second Vatican Council initiated a renovation in the Church which is still going on, and will continue. Some people persist in saying that it was all a mistake, that they should have left the Church the way it was even if it was old-fashioned. Still others have abandoned the Church entirely. But it was the Holy Spirit himself who actually made the decision to update the Church in incidentals while keeping it the same in essentials.

Reliable

Today we should pray for the grace to see that the Holy Spirit was right. We should ask for the vision to see that amid all the uncertainties and anxieties brought on by a too rapidly changing world we have something that is truly stable and reliable, something that can continue to give meaning and purpose to life, something which is essentially the same as it was almost two thousand years ago when it came from Jesus Christ himself and will remain essentially the same until Jesus Christ comes again in glory. That something is our Catholic Religion.

C. E. M.

Sixteenth Sunday of the Year

COME AND REST

Modern day means of communication are nothing short of fabulous. In a matter of seconds we can know not only what is happening on the other side of the world but even on the moon itself. It is almost impossible to realize that we have actually seen live television pictures from so far out in space. Yes, modern means of communication are fabulous, and yet they pose a threat to each one of us. With their ever present stimuli through sight and sound they can be detrimental to much needed peace and quiet.

Distractions

The average American adult ingests between ten and twenty thousand words a day in newspapers and magazines. He listens to the radio for about seventy-five minutes a day. He is awakened by a clock radio, tunes in while driving his car, and falls asleep at night as an automatic switch turns off the radio next to his bed. In addition he spends several hours each day watching television, more on the weekends especially during the football season.* The result is that while we are rushing to keep up with a world moving at terrific speed, we may in our haste just pass by the whole meaning and purpose of life because we have almost no time to think. We may look back with smiles on another, simpler generation of Americans who had little better to do on a hot, July evening than sit on the front porch, rocking back and forth

---

* Statistics are taken from the book, *Future Shock*, by Alvin Toffler, published by Random House.

BREAKING THE BREAD

in a favorite chair, trying to catch a breath of fresh air outside a stuffy, un-air-conditioned house. Whether the people of that never-to-return era used their time well, we do not know, but at least they had the opportunity for a little peace and quiet, a precious opportunity which we all need desperately to create for ourselves.

False Values

The communications media can do more than simply destroy an opportunity to think. They can and often do exercise a tremendous influence over our value judgments. Consider for a moment the many commercials to which we are exposed and which are so much a part of contemporary life. It is generally agreed that advertising is a necessary element in a competitive economy. Its honest purpose is to supply a choice among products, but many commercials are unabashedly designed to create desire rather than satisfy needs. In their pitch they frequently rely on base human motivation, as we see sex exploited, social status exalted, and economic advancement canonized. The average American is exposed to about 560 commercial messages every day, most of which are calculated to make him dissatisfied with what he has and induce him to want the new, the bigger, the better product. To be open about it, most commercials cater to gross selfishness.

Sunday Mass

Consider now in contrast how little time is dedicated to God here in church. Sunday Mass absorbs about fifty minutes once a week—less time than most of us spend in listening to the radio each day and vastly less time than most of us consume in front of the television set every evening. Is it any wonder that we don't remember from week to week

Sixteenth Sunday of the Year

what we have heard in the scriptures at Mass? Should we be surprised if even an occasionally good homily has little or no effect on our lives? The word of God faces unfair competition for our attention.

Antidote

The communications media have a potential for good. We can and should derive benefit from them by way of entertainment and information. The point is we need an antidote to counteract their potential poison. Today's gospel is not without a suggestion. We saw Jesus surrounded by a large crowd of people say to his apostles, "Come by yourselves to an out-of-the-way place and rest a little." No one had a more important and urgent mission than did Jesus, and yet he knew that important things cannot be accomplished without peace of mind, that even urgent matters cannot be handled properly without reflection. Elsewhere in the gospels we are told that he spent whole nights in prayer, alone with his heavenly Father. He never feared that those hours, carefully, almost stealthily taken from his labors, were wasted. He cherished such hours as absolutely necessary and he tried to teach his apostles the same sense of balance.

Solitude

We need to learn a like sense of balance. Battered as we are by almost ceaseless noise and distraction, we run the risk of wandering aimlessly through life like sheep without a shepherd. Subtly influenced by commercials, to which we would like to think we pay but scarce attention, we may be nurturing selfishness rather than rooting it out. We need to de-stimulate our senses, to lessen the constant flow of sound and images into a weary brain. We must not be afraid of silence, as we force ourselves to turn off the radio, the stereo, the television, and put down our newspapers and magazines—at least during *some* time of the day. We don't have to play the radio *every* time we get into the car. We don't have to have the TV on *all* evening. We must search for solitude and an opportunity to think and pray. Alone with God we should ask ourselves where we are going, what we are trying to accomplish, whether we are using the principles taught by Jesus to solve our problems and shape our opinions. Life is too short to live so much of it in a state of distraction. Time is too precious to spend so little of it in reflecting on what really matters.

The Good Shepherd

The Lord is our Shepherd who wishes to lead us in right paths (responsorial psalm). To follow the Lord we have to be able to hear him. From time to time at least we have to deliberately and of set purpose tune out the noise and distractions of our communications media so that we can tune in to the voice of the Good Shepherd.

C. E. M.

Seventeenth Sunday of the Year

SIGNS AND THE EUCHARIST

Today we began the reading of the sixth chapter of the gospel according to St. John. Since the chapter is very long, seventy-one verses to be exact, the Church has divided it over five successive Sundays. Lengthy though the chapter is, it forms a whole, its theme being the need for faith in Jesus and in his promise of the Eucharist.

Feeding of Five Thousand

As the story begins, we see that Jesus was followed by a very large crowd as he came to the shore of the Sea of Galilee. Jesus had attracted the people because of the miracles he had been working for the sick, but as evening grew on Jesus became aware of a very ordinary, practical problem. The people had nothing to eat, and for most of them a long journey back home still lay before them. Of course in those days there was no question of simply stopping off at a restaurant or hamburger stand along the way. Jesus took upon himself the responsibility of feeding the people. He did so in a miraculous way.

We should not get all involved in just how Jesus worked the miracle. Speculation on the manner of the miracle takes up where the gospel leaves off, for the gospel tells us what happened, not how. Moreover, though it is true that Jesus worked the miracle out of a motive of compassion for the crowd, his concern went deeper than their need for physical nourishment. In fact, St. John does not even mention the motive of compassion—it is a conclusion we draw ourselves.

BREAKING THE BREAD

Rather he speaks of the miracle as a sign, something intended to make his readers think of a reality other than ordinary bread and physical nourishment. That something is the Eucharist. St. John says that Jesus took the loaves of bread and "gave thanks." The Greek word he used for "gave thanks" was the very word which, even when he wrote the gospel, was already the name used for the Blessed Sacrament, "Eucharist." Also St. John noted that the feast of the Passover was near. The notation is more than an indication of the time of the year, for the Passover feast was celebrated with a liturgical meal which was the memorial of the salvation of the Jews from slavery in Egypt. That liturgical meal was a prefigurement, a kind of preview, of the Eucharist. It was later during a Passover supper that Jesus instituted his own Paschal sacrifice, the Eucharist, as a living memorial of our salvation from sin by means of his death and resurrection. St. John presented the feeding of the five thousand, then, as a sign that Jesus wanted to feed his countless followers with a spiritual food in a memorial meal by means of the Eucharist.

Power over Bread

On the day following the feeding of the five thousand Jesus would make his first promise of the Eucharist. That promise would indeed be extraordinary, a real test of faith in Jesus. The miracle of the loaves was a sign well suited to prepare the people to hear these words of Jesus: "The bread that I will give is my flesh for the life of the world." In the miracle Jesus showed that he had power over material elements, bread in particular. As he used his power to feed five thousand people with only five loaves of bread, so he would use his power to change bread into his body to feed multitudes spiritually throughout the ages.

Seventeenth Sunday of the Year

Walking on the Water

There was still another sign to follow that of the miraculous feeding of the five thousand. When the people realized what Jesus had done for them, they wanted to make him king with the idea that with Jesus as their leader they would never have to do a day's work again. He could go on feeding them miraculously. Jesus of course did not want to be that kind of a king, and so he hid from the people. No one could find him. His disciples guessed that he would eventually show up in Capernaum on the other side of the lake, his headquarters at the time, and so they got into their boat and started across the lake. When they had rowed three or four miles, to their utter amazement they sighted Jesus approaching the boat, walking on the water.

Walking on the water was another sign in preparation for the promise of the Eucharist, for Jesus showed that he had power over his own body, a power that he would use in making his body truly present under the appearances of bread. The next day the people found out what had happened because they knew that there was only one boat and that Jesus did not get into that boat, and yet had reached the other side. Undoubtedly they made inquiries, and it was then that they heard what Jesus had done.

Our Faith

As we shall see on a later Sunday, even these tremendous signs were not enough for most of the people to respond with assent to the promise of the Eucharist. Why they failed to accept the truth that Jesus would give his flesh to eat, we simply do not know. But the account of these two signs, the feeding of the five thousand and the walking on the water, has been recorded in the gospel to bolster our faith in this great mystery of our religion. These signs, even if we were to witness them personally today, cannot give us faith, for faith is a gift from God. But their proclamation in the gospel today should serve as an occasion for us to readily renew our faith in the Eucharist. We can make the words of today's responsorial psalm a beautiful expression of that faith: "The hand of the Lord feeds us; he answers all our needs." The eyes of the faithful look hopefully to the Lord, and he gives the spiritual food of the Eucharist. Please stand—and let us all repeat in faith the words: "The hand of the Lord feeds us; he answers all our needs."

C. E. M.

Eighteenth Sunday of the Year

FAITH COMES FROM A HEARTY APPETITE

Appetite has always been a barometer of health. When someone is "off his feed," he is not feeling too well. And more seriously, we worry when an elderly person or someone suffering from alcoholism doesn't feel like eating. Strength diminishes as the appetite does. But in a happier sense, picture the traditional joy of a mother feeding the "lumberjack" pangs of her growing children. And more than one bride (sharing a recipe with her mother-in-law) has become convinced that the way to a man's heart is through his stomach.

Jewish Diners

It's easy to suspect that the way to the Jewish hearts of the first century seems to have been through their stomachs. After multiplying bread, our Lord had an eager audience. But it was the kind of audience that's grabbing but not listening. And so our Lord gave the rebuff: have faith not in manna (which is looking to the past), not in the luncheon loafs (with minimum strength for the present), but have faith in me, the Bread of Life.

Vivacious Circle

The kindness of Christ's admonition for us today is that in spite of our being somewhat unworthy, he trusts our motives and gives himself to us in communion. He gives the gift that improves our motives and expands our appetite for him. Most of us are hungry for Christ and want what he has to offer.

BREAKING THE BREAD

And this appetite for Christ is as good a way as any to describe faith. In the divine circle, the more we are hungry for Christ, the more fulfilling is the Eucharistic Bread. And the more satisfying our experience of Christ in communion, the stronger our faith becomes, and the more frequently and fervently we seek Christ.

Not Saints

The saints with their hunger for Christ are much more satisfied and filled with the Eucharistic Lord than we are. We're not saints. We may even be at the zero point. We really need more faith and are starving for it. Lost pilgrims or campers start out looking for directions, friends, and home. But as things get worse, their longing is simply for food. So after a while, if we're really bad off, our longing for identity, success, acceptance gives way to a simple longing for some permanent food: Christ. But we have to allow our hunger-faith appetite to grow. If we're not faith-hungry, then like a sick person we won't find Christ very appealing.

New Man

But how can we acquire a greater appetite for Christ? "Lay aside your former way of life and the old self which deteriorates through illusion and desire, and acquire a fresh, spiritual way of thinking. You must put on the new man...." And put on the new man by having "faith in the one God has sent." We know faith in a friend comes and grows through experience together. We lean on him for support, share our problems and in time, faith is there. It's the same with Christ. We ought to lean on him, share our burdens, communicate with him. Bad day at the office, noisy kids, uninterested parents ought to be shared. What better time than when we have co-union with Christ in the Eucharist? Our new man

Eighteenth Sunday of the Year

has burdens and longs for Christ. So we share the load at communion time with the Lord and satisfy the longing for Christ by receiving the Eucharistic Bread. The more we share, the better the friendship. The more we eat, the greater the fulfillment of his presence. More friendship and greater fulfillment bring stronger faith.

The problem for many early listeners and perspective believers of Christ was that they had faith only in bread, not in him, just as their ancestors had faith in manna and quail, but not in the Father who provided the nourishment. Our Bread is bound to evoke stronger feelings of faith for us, since it is Christ himself. Better than discovering a diamond in a piece of rock, better than money found in a tin can, we find in the Eucharistic Bread Jesus Christ, God himself. And more than being an "eternal meal ticket," Christ is the friend to share the journey, remove hunger and thirst, and fulfill the appetite's wildest fancies. Give the Eucharist a try. The taste is divine.

M. M. R.

Nineteenth Sunday of the Year

FOOD FOR TRAVELING

Funerals are obviously difficult times in anyone's life. Especially so for a priest or minister who hopes in some way to console the family of the deceased. Psychologists try to soften the professional burden by suggesting that it doesn't matter too much what you say to the family. Their shock doesn't allow much listening. What does help is that the concerned priest is present to share some of the grief. But while this may be true of a shocked family (not hearing specific words) a counsellor wants to be saying something, not just at a funeral, but whenever death comes up.

Christ's Words

Fortunately and blessedly, a priest can simply say "Christ is life." Death is the lonely step seen from our end of the dark valley. But for the dead person, this is the grandest step of his life. And the ease of counselling almost doubles if the person has been able to attend Mass regularly and has received the Eucharist. "I am the bread from heaven. If anyone eats this bread he shall live forever."

Our Lord's listeners certainly understood the literalness of his words. What they questioned was how could such claims be made by a home town boy. Many men have dreamed of immortality but no one before or after Christ claimed to be food for eternal life.

Role Play

A short time ago two seventh grade CCD students were asked to "role play" the following situation. "John, your best

Nineteenth Sunday of the Year

friend Mark was absent from school. A few days later someone says that Mark was killed in an auto accident in the north. That afternoon you're walking around the shopping center, sad over the loss of your friend, when suddenly you see him—live as can be, standing by a counter. The real story is that Mark went to see his grandmother. The family had a car accident. No one was hurt. All are home now. But you don't know this. All you know is that Mark is dead, but you see him standing there. Now, what do you say to him?"

After stammering and smiling, each of the boys found it very hard to play the role. The whole class found it too hard to do realistically: meeting someone you thought had died. It is hard to imagine life after death. This explains why faith in the resurrection is somewhat difficult. But taking another approach, science tells us that energy can't be annihilated. It's form may change, but it is still around. The human body and personality with its detectable electrical and chemical energy, when it faces death faces a change in its form, but not a destruction of its energy. Christ simply frees us from chemical terms and suggests to us what this life is about.

Power of the Eucharist

The Lord knew what he was talking about. In his own death and resurrection Christ demonstrates the power of the Eucharist to carry us through life and death to our resurrection. With the real presence of Christ, the Eucharist contains the God of Ages, the Lord of Life. And in receiving Communion early in life, we receive the seed of immortality. Through the years we begin to live the resurrection, growing day by day, year by year until its full unfolding at our death.

Poison

But this process of eternal life isn't automatic. Paul tells us we can slow down this ascent to life. Bitterness, passion,

BREAKING THE BREAD

anger, harsh words, not only "kill" others but stunt our growing and can even suffocate the life within us. So we have to be careful to feed this life with the Eucharist Bread and keep a road map in mind for where this life is taking us. Fortunately we're not looking for broom trees and death; we're traveling to find the Father. And no one has seen the Father except Christ. So Our Lord knows what we need. He eagerly gives us the bread to carry on our journey to the Father. And happily the Eucharist carries us far beyond forty days. It carries us on to the end and the beginning beyond. Taste, and with the coming of death, see the goodness of the Lord.

M. M. R.

Solemnity of the Assumption

Suggested use: **Penitential Rite C**

You have come to give us abundant life,
Lord have mercy.

You gave your mother eternal life,
Christ have mercy.

You promise us eternal life,
Lord have mercy.

ABUNDANT LIFE

Today's celebration of the Assumption, together with its ennobling and uplifting scriptural readings, stands in striking contrast with a mood of our times. All around us we see apathy, depression, pessimism. Frustrations and disappointments seem to be endless and yet leading nowhere. Even many young people, caught in a world of conflict and confusing change, are giving up on life.

Promise of Life

What a pity these young people, and those who once were young, cannot experience the meaning of the abundant life which Christ promised and gave to his mother. Our celebration of Mary's Assumption body and soul into eternal life should help all of us feel the worth of every effort to live life to the full here and now. Only in this way can we hope to live life to the full eternally. The cynic will probably respond to today's feast with its promise of life by saying that it is all nice poetry and fancy but a far cry from reality with all its harshness and drabness. Well, a lot depends on one's view of reality. Mary's view can be summarized in the opening words of her song of praise as found in today's gospel: "My being proclaims the greatness of the Lord, my spirit finds joy in God my savior."

A Mistake

One big mistake some people make is that they try to get through life on their own. They think that religion is a sign of weakness, a crutch, and they prefer to stand on their own two feet. They are proud. But Mary was humble. She exclaimed: "God has looked upon his servant in her lowliness; God who is mighty has done great things for me." She knew that all her privileges came from God, and that his power alone was making her life worthwhile. She went through her life, with all its problems and difficulties, in a spirit of complete trust in God. She had to see her son leave their home in Nazareth to begin his public ministry. With a mother's sympathy, she shared in the ridicule, the disdain, and the rejection which her son had to endure. She stood on Calvary and witnessed her son die a criminal's death. And through it all she never gave up on life, for her trust was not in herself but in God.

Reality

Was Mary's trust misplaced? Were her hopes only fantasy? Certainly not! Because Mary trusted that the Lord's words to her would be fulfilled, she was raised body and soul to the abundance of life. Her son had drawn human life from her womb, but she drew eternal life from his death on the cross. Like Mary our happiness in life comes from our acceptance of God's promise of life. Like Mary we can draw life from the death of Christ. Our Eucharistic acclamation of faith is: "Dying you destroyed our death; rising you restored our life; Lord Jesus, come in glory."

Solemnity of the Assumption

Look to the Hill

Lew Sarett in his poem, "The World Has a Way with Eyes," after describing the various things a young girl sees, strikes this encouraging note:

> Keep a long, long look on pine and peak that rise
> Serene today, tomorrow—when the world's eyes go
> To socketed dust; keep a long look on the hills.
> They know something, child, they know.

At this moment let us take a long look at the hill of Calvary where Mary stood at the foot of the cross. When Christ opened his arms on the cross, he also opened the door to eternal life for himself, for Mary, and for us. That hill in our own time is the altar. To the altar we come for life here and hereafter.

O. J. M.
C. E. M.

Twentieth Sunday of the Year

IT'S WISE TO EAT

When I was in the seminary and a fine fellow student would "drop out," deciding not to continue to study for the priesthood, I would begin a long process of evaluation. "He's a better student than I am—gets all A's. He's a fine speaker, has a great personality. He'd really wow the people as a priest. Why did he drop out?" I never came up with very good answers. And the passage of years hasn't helped the questioning. Even today the same twinge of examination pops up when a priest I know decides not to remain in the priesthood. And this situation isn't unique to the priesthood. How many married couples—so ideally suited (we thought) are having trouble staying together, while the mixed-matched defy all predictions and are happily married? How many "bad'" kids grow up and become great people, while their talented peers can't find a place in life?

Mystery

It all would be baffling except that through these experiences an awareness evolves. You become aware that there is a subtle wisdom guiding events in the world. It obviously isn't my wisdom. All my "winners" seem to be walking out. Word gets around about a priest who is marvelous with the sick, or small children, and his classmates remember what a poor student he was in the seminary. The unsuited couple become wonderful parents. Or the child who wouldn't amount to much goes off to join Vista. The book of Proverbs gently gives us clues for these events. "Let whoever is simple turn in here." God's wisdom has all things worked out. And he generally uses the simple to confound the wise.

Epicenter

And the confrontation of human and divine wisdom can be best seen in the Eucharist. Human judgment declares it only bread. After all, be reasonable. How could it be anything else? Divine judgment declares: the bread that I give is my flesh for the life of the world.

The extension of God among men is called wisdom throughout the Old Testament. One could almost substitute "Christ" in the first reading today for the word "wisdom." Christ in the first reading does invite us: "Come eat my food and drink the wine I have mixed: forsake foolishness that you may live, advance in the way of understanding." Paul is just as insistent: "Do not act like fools, but like thoughtful men. Make the most of the present opportunity."

Reaction

And this is where the nonchristian listeners of the Lord went astray. They understood clearly Christ's offer of flesh to eat. But their "profound" human wisdom told them this could not be. So they were foolish enough to pass up life itself.

If your faith is confused these days, listen to Christ: to him who lacks understanding, I say, come eat my food. If you have worries about the Church, the vocation crisis, the condition of the world today, come eat my food. If your problems and disappointments make little sense, come eat my food. Don't rely on your own wisdom to save the world, try to dis-

BREAKING THE BREAD

cern the will of the Lord. And come eat my food, and drink the wine I have mixed. Forsake foolishness that you may live; advance in the way of understanding. Then real wisdom will come to you: Christ himself.

M. M. R.

Twenty-First Sunday of the Year

WILL YOU STAY?

On a number of Sundays now Christ has been speaking about giving himself to us in the Eucharist. And today he finally asks: Do you accept this? Do you really appreciate what I have been telling you about Communion, or have you considered me like a car salesman on TV: it's too much to take seriously? Would it be easier to leave politely rather than have to give an answer, rather than have to live up to the reality of the Eucharist?

An Example

To live up to the Eucharist means among other things seeing that through the Eucharist people become one with Christ. Paul gives us one fine example, or application, and he isn't speaking mere poetry. He's talking about some of the effects of seeing others as one with Christ through the Eucharist. If a wife sees her husband as "eucharistic," she will offer respect to him. If a husband sees his wife as "eucharistic," he will give himself for her. They will do this totally, caring for each other as they do their own bodies. "This sort of talk is hard to endure; how can anyone take it seriously?" Remember when you used to hear that "marriages are made in heaven?" Maybe the saying would better be: no one comes to union with another except through Christ and no one comes to Christ unless brought by the heavenly Father.

The Church

Husbands and wives are the Church in miniature, an expression of the "eucharistic" people of God. They can give a sample of how we should care for each other and remind us that Christ's deep love for us is best seen in this total kind of love. Love is care, protection, respect, and growth.

To accept the fact that we are all bound to this type of love is difficult, but we must do so if we really want to accept the Eucharist. The teachings of Christ through the Church on divorce or abortion are easily digested when they don't apply to us. But for the poor parent and three children abandoned by the spouse, for the young girl discovering pregnancy outside marriage, the talk of the Church is hard to endure, especially when not too many today are taking these words seriously.

Faith

Would even the experience of seeing Christ in his glory, a vision of heaven, make some life situations any easier? Probably not. A strong spirit has to fill us, the spirit of Christ that comes to us through the Eucharist. It is a spirit which gives strength to a married person to live singly, for a young girl to have her child and then offer it for adoption. They are many who don't think the Church's teaching is important. It's just too hard to accept.

Yet Christ gives us the Eucharistic food, the strength to make difficult decisions. He gives us his presence as a friend. The Lord is close to the brokenhearted. He gives us his spirit as counsellor to see wisdom. But all this helps only if we believe. Some of the Jews left Christ because they could not believe in the Eucharist. But husbands and wives and families with faith can stay together and remain in the Church because of the Eucharist as well. Each of us can find help to cope with problems, even be heroic. And we ought to turn to assist those around us who have still greater problems.

Twenty-First Sunday of the Year

The Question

Let Joshua ask the question during this Mass, "If it does not please you to serve the Lord, decide today whom you will serve." Beg Christ to help you with your answer. "Lord, there may be days when I'm tempted to walk out, but to whom shall I go? You have the words of eternal life. We have come to believe; we are convinced that you are God's holy One."

M. M. R.

Twenty-Second Sunday of the Year

OF LIPS AND HEARTS

At first hearing, today's gospel sounds like a scene from a family dinner table. How many parents have asked their children as they sat down to eat, "Did you wash your hands?" The Pharisees had observed some of the disciples of Jesus eating meals without having washed their hands. Their concern, however, was not with hygiene but with religious practice. Originally, symbolic purification had been connected with the Jewish liturgy, somewhat after the present practice of the priest washing his hands during the Mass. By custom over the centuries that ritual washing was extended to circumstances of everyday life and in the minds of people like the Pharisees had taken on an importance out of all proportion to the value of the act.

Easy Religion

Jesus objected strenuously to the attitude of the Pharisees. It was not that the washing was a bad thing. What was bad was the notion that such formal and merely external actions constituted a person's religion, to the exclusion of what was really important as an expression of piety. Insistence on such actions had taken all the heart out of religion. The people had received God's commandments through Moses and had been told to observe them carefully (first reading), but it was a lot easier and less demanding for a Jew to wash his hands than it was to love God with his whole being and his neighbor as himself. Perhaps a parallel situation is the fact that it is a lot easier for us to say grace before meals than it is to be kind and considerate, without bickering or arguing, during the meal. Saying grace is good, but to think that it alone, with no attempt to show love for those with whom we eat, makes us religious is to fall into the error of the Pharisees.

Pharisaism?

Perhaps we have been more Pharisaical in some of our Catholic practices than we would like to admit. In recent times a lot of our customs have become little more than history. Most of us can recall that a "practical" Catholic was one who was at Mass every Sunday, went to confession and Communion at least once a month, never ate meat on Friday and wore a medal. These criteria, these norms for being a "good" Catholic, were not bad. They were, however, dangerous because they could, and sometimes did, lead to complacency in religion. Some people regret that the old external signs of piety are being lost, but let's try to be honest about this problem without putting up our defenses. Isn't it true that it has been relatively easy to get to Mass every Sunday? There was sometimes a pride in refusing to eat meat on a Friday in the company of non-Catholics, but the sacrifice involved was really not very much. Getting to confession regularly involved more effort—an effort which, incidentally, some of us should be using again—but perhaps our confessions were vague and more a case of routine than an expression of true sorrow with sincere repentance. And the wearing of a medal did not make us a good Catholic any more than putting a patriotic bumper sticker on a car makes the driver a good American.

Keeping Perspective

Please do not misunderstand me. I am not saying that you should not come to Mass every Sunday or wear a medal. My point—the point of Jesus in the gospel—is that merely external practices do not make us religious. We can never overemphasize this truth. In fact, we are even now in danger of falling into another form of externalism in our manner of celebrating the Mass. This is what I mean. Singing the hymns and saying the prayers aloud within the Mass are important. Anyone who does not think so has not been listening to the official teaching of the Church. But if we do these things without attention and devotion and a sincere attempt to express real love for God, we may very well hear God say: "This people pays me lip service, but their heart is far from me." Much more of the Bible is being read as part of the Mass, and yet hearing the word of God is not enough. As St. James tells us in the second lesson: "Act on this word. If all you do is listen to it, you are deceiving yourselves." Most Catholics these days are receiving Holy Communion every Sunday, and that is a very good thing, but if we are not making an effort to grow more like Christ in our lives, we are neglecting one of the purposes of Communion. Moreover, if we think that we can express love for God here at Mass, and then go out and make no attempt to show love for his children by trying to overcome the misery and injustices which are part of our society, we are modern-day Pharisees.

Not Easy

The Pharisees had missed the meaning of religion. There is no easy, external thing we can do to guarantee our being devout. God asks for a devotion which involves our whole being. In the words of today's responsorial psalm, God wants us to walk blamelessly and do justice, to think the truth in our hearts and slander not with our tongue, to harm not our fellow man. He requires a piety which involves not only our prayers but also our actions, not only our lips but also our hearts.

C. E. M.

Twenty-Third Sunday of the Year

TO HEAR AND TO SPEAK

After a very long illness a woman completely lost her hearing. Apparently a virus had destroyed the auditory nerve in both ears. It was like cutting the wire on a telephone; she was totally deaf. She went from specialist to specialist in search of a cure, but she always received the same answer: medical science had not yet found a way to replace the damaged nerve. Finally a man posing as a doctor promised that he could cure her by means of hypnosis, and the woman paid him ten thousand dollars, every penny she owned. Unfortunately the man was a charlatan, a quack. He took her money and that was the last she ever saw of him.

Human Faculties

The fact that the woman was willing to pay so much money to regain her hearing points up how much we value our human faculties—once we have lost them. If we try to put ourselves in the place of the man in today's gospel, I think we can begin to appreciate his predicament. The man was deaf. Try to imagine what that means: to be cut off entirely from the whole world of sound. In a moment of danger a human voice could not warn him. In a time of sorrow a human voice could not console him. The laughter of children, the conversation of friends, the joy of music— these were not a reality for him. And as a consequence of his deafness he could not speak plainly, for he could not hear himself. He found it almost impossible to let others know how he felt or what he wanted. He could not express his emotions or his feelings. He lived in a world almost completely cut off from the people with whom he lived.

The Miracle

You can understand, then, his joy and enthusiasm when Jesus cured him. What a great day that was for him! Do you think he ever forgot it as long as he lived? Engraven on his memory was every detail: the time of day, the place, the weather, everything. Even the bystanders were so impressed that, as the gospel says, "their amazement knew no bounds."

Our Faculties

It is only natural that we should take for granted our ability to hear and our ability to speak. It is natural, but it is not right. These are great powers for which we must be grateful, and the best way to be grateful is by using these powers as God intended. The power to speak is one of the faculties which separates us from animals. We abuse this power when we use it to tell an untruth, to spread ugly rumors or demeaning gossip. Speech is intended to communicate truth and goodness, not lies and hatred. Our hearing too is to be used judiciously, not as an encouragement to another's abuse of his speech by lending our willing ear. Moreover, both our speech and our hearing are meant for something even higher than human communication. They are also our means of communicating with God. The rite of baptism brings out this higher use.

Baptism

When we were baptized the priest touched our ears, saying the very word used by Jesus to cure the deaf man: "Ephphatha!" This was a sign that our ears should be opened

Twenty-Third Sunday of the Year

not merely to the words of our fellow men but also to the word of God. It meant that we should hear the word of God in faith. Faith opens our ears spiritually. Other people may hear the word of God in a physical way, that is, they may listen to the reading of the Bible, but without faith they do not hear that word as God's communication. They are, for one reason or another, spiritually deaf, as we ourselves were without the gift of faith received in baptism.

The Mass

In the Mass we hear the word of God in the scriptures and in the homily. We must try to open our ears in faith and listen attentively. Once we hear the word of God in faith, we must then respond by means of our power of speech. Once we believe in God, we must praise him, thank him, ask him for what we need, and express our sorrow for our sins. We must make a real effort to participate with intelligence and devotion in the prayers and hymns.

I am sure that the deaf man in the gospel really appreciated his powers after he had been cured. Today we should pray God to give us an appreciation of what we have: first, for our power to speak to each other, as well as for our power to speak to God in prayer; secondly, for our ability to hear each other, as well as for our ability to hear the word of God in faith.

Free Gift

The woman who had lost her hearing because of a virus was willing to pay ten thousand dollars for a cure. God cured our spiritual deafness by means of baptism, and it was a gift. It is a gift we should never forget or take for granted.

C. E. M.

Twenty-Fourth Sunday of the Year
Suggested Use: **Fourth Eucharistic Prayer**

MAKE UP YOUR MIND

Richard Cardinal Cushing is credited with the following recipe for renewal.

If all the sleeping folks will wake up,
And all the lukewarm folks will fire up,
And all the dishonest folks will confess up,
And all the disgruntled folks will sweeten up,
And all the discouraged folks will cheer up,
And all the depressed folks will look up,
And all the estranged folks will make up,
And all the gossipers will shut up,
And all the dry bones will shake up,
And all the true soldiers will stand up,
And all the Church members will pray up —
THEN you can have the world's greatest renewal.

Bring It to a Boil

I cannot say if Cardinal Cushing got his inspiration from the Vatican Council or not. Anyway, Martin H. Work, commenting on the Decree on the Apostolate of the Laity published by the Second Vatican Council, has these remarks.

"Although a 'lay apostolate' has existed in the Church since the days of our Lord in Jerusalem, it was not until the Second Vatican Council that the Church's official thinking on the matter was stated in a conciliar decree. As one layman put it pungently, 'The lay apostolate has been simmering on the 'back burner' of the Church's apostolic life for nearly two thousand years, and finally the Fathers of this Council moved it up to the 'front burner' and 'turned the heat up all the way.' Everyone hopes it will 'come to a boil' soon because so much of the Church's mission depends on an apostolic laity."

Twenty-Fourth Sunday of the Year

Since Vatican II we have been moving in the direction of bringing the lay apostolate "to a boil." The readings in this Mass urge us to continue working in this direction. For "the renewal of the Church depends in great part on a laity that fully understands ... their own co-responsibility for the mission of Christ in the Church and in the world" (Martin Work).

Who Do We Say Christ Is?

The question Jesus addressed to his disciples is the same one he addresses to us. Our baptism brought us into contact with Christ and his saving grace. As we grow up and come to the maturity that allows us to make responsible decisions, it is necessary to make up our minds about Jesus Christ. "If a man wishes to come after me, he must deny his very self, take up his cross, and follow in my steps." This is a decision that must reflect what Isaiah prophesies of Christ as we have it in the first reading. "I have not rebelled, have not turned back." Our response to this first reading, "I will walk in the presence of the Lord," is a further affirmation of our decision to go with Christ. When we seek for solutions to the problems of our society, we must say with Peter, "You are the Messiah." It is foolish to look for salvation for ourselves or society in general in anyone except Christ.

Not Merely "Don'ts"

Our decision to follow Christ is only half fulfilled when we live our lives only according to "don'ts." Eddie observed all the "don'ts," but he gave very little attention to the "do's." He never stole from anyone, but neither did he go out of his way to contribute to those who are hungry. Eddie could not be accused of cheating the other fellow, and yet you couldn't say that Eddie was generous in lending a helping hand. And

BREAKING THE BREAD

that's the whole way Eddie's life went—a person living his life in only half measure. St. James in the second reading today is rather forceful on the minimum value of living your life on the negative side. "If a brother or sister has nothing to wear and no food for the day, and you say to them, 'Good-bye and good luck! Keep warm and well fed,' but do not meet their bodily needs, what good is that?" Incidentally, Eddie never misses Mass, but, then, he never participates either.

Positive Following of Christ

The following of Christ demands positive action. We have to make up our minds to let his words and actions have a definite influence in all the decisions we make. We must show positive works, and the faith that underlies those works. It will cost us sufferings of various kinds to be a full Christian. "Christ began to teach his disciples that the Son of Man had to suffer much." If we will be Christ in the world—and this is the apostolate of the layman—then we must expect to suffer. And if we are not willing to do this, then we cannot hope to renew the world in Christ. So, as Christians, we need to take a stand on violence, brutality, the killing of the innocent, the damaging of private property, and public, too. War, as it is fought today, cannot be tolerated, much less glorified. The hatred of labor for management must stop. Yes, abuses must be corrected, but in a spirit of genuine brotherly love. As a Christian, I cannot sit idly by and watch millions of fellow human beings starving because of politics. The list could go on and on. But let me conclude. Before I do, please do not "cop out" on your Christian responsibility by asking for someone to show you what to do. The only One to ask, really, is the Spirit of God, and He it is whom we invoke in this Mass. To summarize, let's hear once again Cardinal Cushing's "if's." (*Read again the opening paragraph*).

O. J. M.

Twenty-Fifth Sunday of the Year[1]

PEOPLE ARE PRECIOUS

When many of us were children we were often reminded that children should be seen and not heard. That was a way of telling us that children had a place and that they had better learn to keep it. The "place" was perhaps not very exalted in the minds of some, but in our Lord's own day children were underprivileged indeed. They enjoyed no clear rights in society. They were almost totally dependent on the good will of their elders, and were treated quite impersonally, like an "it" rather than a "he."[2]

Surprise

The scene in today's gospel is a very touching one. Jesus took a little child and put his arms around him. The words that followed, however, came as a shock to the disciples: "Whoever welcomes a child such as this for my sake welcomes me." Were children suddenly to become very important people? Was there to be an almost complete change in the way children were regarded? Yes, that is what Jesus was demonstrating for his disciples both by his words and by his actions. But Jesus wanted to teach a more extensive lesson: if even a child, this "it" of that day's society, must be treated with

---

1. Both last Sunday's gospel and today's contain a prediction of the passion. Moreover, today's declaration, "If anyone wishes to rank first, he must remain the last one of all and the servant of all," finds a more complete treatment in the gospel for the Twenty-Ninth Sunday of the Year. The homily presented here, therefore, concentrates on the theme of welcoming even a child.
2. Bruce Vawter, C.M., *The Four Gospels*, p. 206.

respect and love, then *every* human being must be treated with respect and love. Jesus was saying in effect that all people are important: big people and little people, rich people and poor people, clean people and dirty people, black people and white people.

Reason

Jesus gave a reason why all people are important: he said, "Whoever welcomes a child ... welcomes me." The Book of Genesis teaches us that God made man in his own image and likeness. That image, that idea which God has is a Person, God the Son. Human beings are made in the image and likeness of God the Son. This conformity to God the Son is the first and primary source of their dignity and worth.[3] Moreover, God the Father sent his son into the world to be human like us in all things except sin, and thereby elevated and sanctified human life. God demands respect for human beings as he demands respect for his own son.

Respect for human life is quickly being reduced in our society. The reason is that we are experiencing a creeping atheism all around us, not just a theoretical atheism which says there is no God but more significantly a practical atheism which acts as if there is no God. Without God there is no sound basis for human dignity. Christianity teaches that man is made a little less than the angels, but atheism puts man in a position which is little better than that of animals.

Abortion

There are several symptoms of the effect of creeping atheism. The first of these is the abortion movement. No

---

3. The doctrine of the Mystical Body is also a foundation for the teaching of Jesus, but its introduction in this context would leave open in the minds of the people the status of those who in no way are part of the Mystical Body of Christ.

Twenty-Fifth Sunday of the Year

informed person in his right mind can pretend that the child in the womb is not a human being. Science has proven that the product of human conception is a human being right from the beginning, that human life is a continuum from conception until death.[4] But if the child is not made in the image and likeness of God, why should anyone worry about him? If that child is not of great worth in the sight of God, why should anyone inconvenience himself for the sake of that child? No one is going to make any considerable sacrifice to safeguard the life of an alley cat, but without God an unborn child is but little better than an animal.

Racial Prejudice

Take the problem of racial prejudice. Why shouldn't I look down on other people if I do not believe that God has created all men equal? There would be no need for civil rights' organizations if we all lived according to the words of the Declaration of Independence which states "that man has been endowed by the Creator with certain inalienable rights." The problem of parental authority fits into the same context. There is no real reason for a child to respect and obey his parents if he does not believe that God has created him through those parents. Atheism implies that conception and birth are biological accidents, not the work of God. Moreover, when a parent tries to persuade his child that he should not use dope, there is no good argument without God. If a human person has no divinely given dignity, why shouldn't he do with his body whatever he wants, even if it be to destroy that body with drugs? And why shouldn't he use another person sexually solely for his own pleasure? How can

---

4. For a simplified presentation of the scientific arguments, cf. "Abortion, Good Science = Good Morals" in the *Homiletic and Pastoral Review* for July 1970. Another presentation can be found in the article, "Abortion: It's Human, So What?" in *Pastoral Life* for April 1971.

BREAKING THE BREAD

there be anything seriously wrong with murder, rape, and all the rest if there is no belief in God?

Real Belief

It is imperative that we overcome creeping atheism in our society. The primary way to do so is not by arguments and debates but by living our faith. As believers in God, as followers of Christ, we must respect all human beings, big people, and little people, rich people and poor people, clean people and dirty people, black people and white people. To do less is to be an atheist in practice if not in theory.

C. E. M.

Twenty-Sixth Sunday of the Year*

STARFISH AND CHRISTIANS

The starfish is a fascinating marine animal. From its central disc radiate five armlike projections. What is so remarkable about the starfish is its ability called autotomy. If some underwater creature has gotten a firm grip on one of its arms, the starfish can break off the captured arm in order to escape to freedom, thereby disappointing its hungry adversary. What is even more remarkable, the starfish can later grow an entirely new arm, a process known as regeneration.

In comparison with starfish we as human beings have only limited powers of regeneration. Cut areas of the skin or a broken bone can be regenerated, but not an entire structure such as an arm or even a finger. You wouldn't mind cutting off a hand or foot or even tearing out an eye if you could simply grow back the missing part. And yet Jesus today in the gospel is talking to us as if we were starfish!

Making a Point

Of course Jesus did not wish to be taken literally. His words about cutting off a hand or foot and tearing out an eye represent a typically Semitic way of making a point by means of exaggeration. But Jesus did want to make a point

---

* Since today's gospel pericope is a collection of Jesus' sayings rather loosely connected and combined by the evangelist through means of verbal associations, it is difficult to treat it as a unified whole. And though the lesson from Numbers focuses on the first verses of the pericope, it seems that the attention of the people would be caught by the later verses which speak of cutting off hands and feet and tearing out eyes.

and he wanted to make it quite emphatically: nothing is more important than eternal salvation; no sacrifice is too great to attain it.

The Jesus we hear in the gospel today seems somewhat out of character with our usual picture of the gentle, loving Savior, the good shepherd, the divine physician. His words sound somber and threatening. Jesus pronounced them, however, only because he does love us and has our eternal welfare at heart. His words contain a truth which from time to time we really need to be reminded of. Heaven is the goal of life; it would be a terrible thing to fail to attain that goal. What a tragic mistake it would be to place anything or anyone above our eternal salvation! Jesus does not want our lives to end in tragedy.

Temptations

Of course we believe that heaven is our goal. If we did not, we wouldn't even bother to be here in church today. And yet isn't it true that sometimes we are tempted to think that we really don't have to be too strict with ourselves, that we can get by with a bare minimum? Or maybe we become envious of people who seem to get along just fine without any kind of moral code as they do whatever they please. Sometimes we may even feel that we are missing something. Perhaps we are like the little child who finds a fascination in matches simply because he has been warned not to play with them.

Tension

There is a certain amount of tension in the life of everyone of us. I am not talking about the anxieties brought on by modern problems, the kind of nervous tension we see depicted in television commercials for "Compoz" and the like.

Twenty-Sixth Sunday of the Year

I am referring to the fact that we are pulled in two directions at the same time—outward toward God and inward toward ourselves. We know that we should lead lives centered on the love of God, that we should be unselfish and loving toward others, but all the while we are tempted to think only of ourselves. If you pick up a rubber band and pull in opposite directions, you create a tension. Once you let go of one end, there is no longer any tension. God is trying to draw us to himself, but we are pulling in the opposite direction. That makes for tension, and consequently unhappiness for us. In one sense, what life is all about is learning to let go from our end.

I can't tell you what you should let go of. Each person has to discover that for himself. He has to honestly admit what it is that is holding him back from God. Then he must pray for the courage to make the necessary sacrifice, to give up anything to find God, even if it be something or someone as precious as a hand, or a foot, or an eye.

Regeneration — Resurrection

When we have let go, we will learn that we have done the right thing. The starfish sacrifices an arm, a temporary disadvantage, so that he can survive and later regenerate a new arm. Actually we are better off than the starfish. We have a much higher form of spiritual regeneration. It is called resurrection. In this Mass we profess our faith in the resurrection of Christ and we express hope for our own resurrection. Any temporary disadvantage we may suffer now as a sacrifice will be more than compensated for. We will rise with Christ to a new, a better life, a life of perfect and complete happiness which will never end.

C. E. M.

Twenty-Seventh Sunday of the Year

GOD'S IDEA OF A LOVE STORY

In many quarters these days there is a concern over the rapidly increasing divorce rate. Some psychologists are pointing out that divorce does not solve problems, but only opens up an avenue of temporary escape, an avenue with a dead end. They observe that after divorce a trauma of failure remains, with loneliness and guilt as constant reminders of what might have been. Family counsellors have long maintained that children need the love and guidance of *both* parents, and they insist that divorce destroys a part of children's birthright and jeopardizes their future happiness. There is a growing awareness, among some at least, that the relaxation of divorce laws is a favor to no one.

Jesus' Stand

In the gospel we saw Jesus take a strong stand against divorce, despite the practice of his day. His stand was unpopular then and it is unpopular today, but he continues to be opposed to divorce. His position on the permanence of marriage is not based on a legalistic approach—on whether there is a law which either forbids or allows divorce. It is not even based primarily on the harm done to children and society by divorce. Rather it is based on the fact that sex and its fulfillment in marriage are God's idea, his creation, and that from the beginning God intended marriage to be a lasting relationship between one man and one woman. Jesus has in mind the beauty and meaning of the sexual relationship as expressed in the words from the book of Genesis, "They are no longer two but one flesh."

Twenty-Seventh Sunday of the Year

Sex Speaks

"They are no longer two but one flesh"—this simple statement, as understood and developed by the long tradition of the Church, means that in God's plan sex is supposed to say something. It is intended to express a relationship so profound that mere words are inadequate for it. Sex says, "I love you completely, exclusively, and forever." "I love you completely—I give myself to you without any holding back, and I accept you just as you are, with all of your wonderful, thrilling qualities as well as with your human shortcomings." Let me speak very plainly but quite seriously. We are clothed here today, not only to keep warm or to follow the styles, but because we do not belong to each other. When a husband and a wife express their sexual love, they appear before each other unclothed, naked, because they hold nothing back, they belong entirely to each other. "I love you exclusively—since I have given myself to you completely, I cannot give myself that way to anyone else. This does not mean that I am not interested or concerned with anyone else, but it does mean that my relationship with you is unique. There is no one in the whole world toward whom I feel as I feel toward you." "I love you forever—you are so precious, so valuable to me, that I never want to lose you."

When you love someone this way, you think that person is really special. But you also think that you are pretty good yourself since you would not want to give something worthless to the person you love uniquely. And since you think you are both very worthwhile people you instinctively wish to see yourselves repeated and continued in others, your children. Children are not an intrusion on married love, but its finest expression and completion.

High Ideal

"I love you completely, exclusively and forever." This represents a very high ideal of love. The relationship God has in mind cannot be entered into lightly or on a temporary basis. And because it is such a high ideal, we should expect to find that the ideal is not easily reached, that there are many failures along the way. Erich Segal in his popular novel, *Love Story*, which became an equally popular Paramount movie, painted a contemporary picture of a relationship as old as the human race. He made famous the statement, "Love means not ever having to say you're sorry." Some people, while admitting a certain beauty in this statement, have objected to it on the grounds that people do hurt the one they love. Real deep love is not something that happens all of a sudden. It is something which must grow, even amid personal shortcomings. When a wound or hurt has been inflicted, it is vital that the wound be treated with real sorrow; otherwise it leaves a permanent scar. Too many scars destroy the beauty of marriage and lead to the divorce court. Loving someone completely, exclusively, and forever demands bigness, a bigness that can say and mean "I'm sorry." You see, sex is rightly rated "X"—adults only. It is for mature, generous, unselfish people.

Prayer

In the Mass we should praise and thank God for the wonderful gift of sex. We should also pray that we and everyone may see what God had in mind when he created sex to be an expression of a love which is complete, exclusive, and forever.

C. E. M.

Twenty-Eighth Sunday of the Year

HAPPINESS AND THE EYE OF A NEEDLE

Almost every little boy at some time has said, "When I grow up I want to be a fireman." How thrilling it seems to stand on the back of a big red truck as it races toward a fire with its sirens sounding and it lights flashing! How dramatic to climb a precarious ladder into a blazing home to rescue a child, carry him to safety, and place him in the arms of his anxious parents! How satisfying to be acclaimed a hero with your picture in the newspaper! Or so it seems to a little boy. For the veteran firefighter the romance has ended long ago. He has made thousands of trips in the middle of the night and climbed as many ladders, breathed immeasurable quantities of poisonous smoke, suffered injuries and burns, and seen his fellow firemen die. He knows better than anyone else why hell is described in terms of fire.

Accomplishment

Many firemen have asked themselves whether it is all worth the limited pay or the expectation of a pension still far in the future. Why does such a man continue in his job? One fireman gave his answer: "I know that I could not do anything else with such a great sense of accomplishment." [1] His answer reflects the spirit of wisdom presented in our first reading today. It is much like the attitude of the nun who was a nurse in a Louisiana hospital for lepers. A man watched her changing bandages on the ulcerated legs of a patient and said, "Sister, I would not do what you do for a

1. *New York Times*, April 29, 1971.

million dollars." The sister, barely looking up, replied, "Neither would I."

Psychologists have conducted studies on the source of the most elusive of human qualities which we call happiness. Their conclusion has been summarized this way: "Happiness is not in proportion to wealth and leisure, but comes with a sense of accomplishment."[2] It is not without reason that we have developed the saying, "Money can't buy happiness." Many widows, despite comfortable financial means, have discovered that with their husbands dead and their children grown they feel that their lives are without purpose and value. They are unhappy. Men have retired hoping to enjoy a life of leisure only to find that there is a hollowness in having nothing worthwhile to do. They are unhappy. Yet people like the fireman and the nun have found happiness, not in wealth or leisure, but in a sense of accomplishment.

Teaching of Jesus

You know, the world did not have to wait for psychologists to determine that happiness does not come from wealth and leisure. Jesus taught that very truth a long time ago. In fact, he repeatedly warned that riches are a threat to achieving eternal happiness in heaven—not the only threat but certainly a major one. That is why he invited the rich man to sell what he had and give to the poor so that he would have treasure in heaven. Throughout the history of the Church some men and women have taken the words of Jesus literally and embraced the vow of poverty. Not every follower of Christ, however, can become a Trappist monk or a cloistered nun, for if everyone did so no one would be left to carry on the ordinary life of society in a Christian manner. And yet everyone can, and must, take as his own the spirit of the words

2. Reported by Dr. Joyce Brothers on the CBS radio network.

of Jesus. Everyone can acquire a sense of detachment from wealth, a realization that money is not the end and goal of life, but only a means for supporting life. From God, with whom all things are possible, everyone can acquire the wisdom to understand that "happiness is not in proportion to wealth and leisure, but comes from a sense of accomplishment."

Eye of the Needle

No one can deny that it is nice to have enough money to do things and go places and not have to worry about making ends meet. Isn't it true, though, that after you have taken a trip or enjoyed some entertainment there is a certain emptiness when it is all over? The pleasure soon fades. But when you do something for someone else, when you have followed the teaching of Jesus to love your neighbor as he has loved you, the satisfaction does last. And the reward will last forever. A camel trying to pass through a needle's eye is no more ludicrous than a greedy person trying to squeeze into the kingdom of heaven. Only by ridding ourselves of the bloated hump of selfishness and the excess baggage of riches can we hope to make it. Practicing Christian love for others, even at the expense of our pocketbook, will make us happy now and will get us through the eye of the needle into the kingdom of God where we will share everlasting happiness with Jesus Christ.

In Memory of Him

In the Eucharist we have a living memorial of the sacrifice of Jesus Christ: his body given up for us and his blood shed for the forgiveness of our sins. That sacrifice was the greatest accomplishment in the history of the world. Today we are celebrating this Mass because of the command of Jesus, "Do this in memory of me." We will keep his command, not only by celebrating the Mass, but also by trying to lead lives which reflect his sacrificial spirit. That spirit led Jesus to lay down his life for all of mankind. It should lead us to be generous and unselfish with others. It is that spirit alone which gives us what we all seek, that elusive quality which we call happiness.

Right Direction

The little boy who says, "When I grow up I want to be a fireman," is at least looking in the right direction. There really is something thrilling, and dramatic, and satisfying in doing good for others generously and unselfishly. There is indeed wisdom in seeing that true happiness, lasting happiness, comes not from wealth and leisure but from a sense of accomplishment.

C. E. M.

Twenty-Ninth Sunday of the Year
Suggested Use: long form of the gospel

THE SERVANT AND HIS SERVANTS

The Pope has many titles: Bishop of Rome, Primate of Italy, Patriarch of the West. But the title most in keeping with his role as the vicar of Jesus Christ is servant of the servants of God. Jesus said, "I have come not to be served but to serve." The dictionary defines a servant as one who exerts himself for the benefit of another. Jesus certainly fulfilled that definition.

Suffering Servant

The first lesson today is from a section of the book of Isaiah known as the Songs of the Suffering Servant. We have just heard the words of God from this section proclaiming, "Through his suffering my servant shall justify many and their guilt he will bear." The Suffering Servant is Israel, the faithful people of the Old Testament, but in a larger sense he is Jesus Christ, who served by giving his life in atonement for sin. To say that Jesus exerted himself for the benefit of others is indeed an understatement. Jesus gave all that he had.

His Followers

The apostles James and John had misunderstood the mission of Jesus as a servant. They thought that he was about to establish a glorious new kingdom in Israel and they wanted to make sure that they had a place of honor. That is what they had in mind when they asked a favor of Jesus, "See to it that we sit, one at your right and the other at your left when you come into your glory." Little did they realize that Jesus would come into his glory only through his sacrificial death, which Jesus referred to as the cup he had to drink, the bath in which he would be immersed. Good Friday came as a terrible shock to James and John, as well as to the other apostles, and it was only in the light of the resurrection on Easter Sunday that they learned the meaning of Jesus' words in today's gospel. Then they realized that as his followers they too had to become servants, exerting themselves for others even to the point of death. James as a matter of fact was beheaded by Herod Agrippa about 44 A.D., the first of the apostles to endure martyrdom. John was not martyred, but he was tortured and exiled to the island of Patmos where he served his fellow Christians until his death.

We Are Servants

It is one thing to appreciate Jesus as a servant and to be grateful for his generosity in our behalf. It is quite another to recognize that we too must be servants, that exerting ourselves for others is the only way to satisfaction and fulfillment in this life as well as the means for attaining everlasting happiness. Last week we heard Jesus proclaim that happiness does not come from money or leisure but from a sense of accomplishment. Today he wants us to see our accomplishments in terms of service to others. Jesus is very much interested in our having the right attitude in what we do.

We may suspect that to become a servant means doing extraordinary favors for others, special good deeds that are outside the area of our everyday occupations. To some extent that suspicion is correct, but on the other hand we must first get the Christian attitude about our ordinary activities. The Second Vatican Council teaches that "while providing the substance of life for themselves and their families, men and women are performing their activities in a way which appropriately benefits society."[1] In other words, as fathers and mothers you should not look upon the care of your families as worthless routine or sheer drudgery. Fulfilling your duties is a way of becoming a true servant and of sharing in the generous spirit that moved Jesus to sacrifice himself for the benefit of the whole world.

Christian Work

Men and women are also engaged in work outside the family. We refer to this work as a job, a word which suggests activity done for others in order to make money. Money must be earned, but we should look upon our jobs as a way of serving our fellow men. This outlook may appear obvious in the vocation of people like doctors, or teachers or social workers, but it is an outlook that should be shared by all in the course of their needful occupations, whether they be bank tellers, sales clerks, truck drivers, or garbage collectors. Again the Vatican Council teaches us "that the norm of human activity is this: "that in accord with the divine plan and will, it should harmonize with the genuine good of the human race, and allow men as individuals and as members of society to pursue their total vocation and fulfill it."[2] Whatever our job is, it has come into being because of needs in society. In meeting those needs we are servants of our fellow men.

As Christians we must learn to look upon our works as our way of fulfilling our vocation to be servants as was Jesus Christ. We too, like the Pope himself, should cherish as our own the title, "servant of the servants of God."

C. E. M.

1. *The Church in the Modern World,* 34.
2. *Ibid.,* 35.

Thirtieth Sunday of the Year
Suggested Use: **Fourth Eucharistic Prayer**

FAITH AND THANKSGIVING

Today's first reading was addressed to Jews who were living in exile in Babylon. Perhaps "existing" in Babylon is a better way to put it, for there they were an oppressed people, slaves in a foreign country far removed from their home in Palestine. During the period of the exile their religious spirit was almost entirely absorbed in a constant plea that God would remember them and set them free. Above all they yearned to return to their own country, to their beloved city of Jerusalem, and especially to their temple of worship. God, in today's reading from Jeremiah, promised that he would indeed free his people and lead them back safely to their homeland. God kept his promise. After he had done so, however, a strange thing happened. The people's appreciation of God's goodness started to erode. They began to drift away from him. While in exile, when they were in great need, they thought of nothing but God. When that need was met, even though they were once again near their temple, they practically forgot all about God.

The Gospel

In today's gospel we encountered, not a whole people in great need, but a single person. Bartimaeus was blind. From St. Mark's vivid description of the incident, we get the distinct impression that he was a young man, not an elderly person whose sight had gradually failed and for whom only a few years of life were left on earth. A whole lifetime lay before him, and yet he was oppressed by his affliction, a slave of constant darkness. It is no wonder that he did not hesitate to make a scene when he heard that Jesus was pass-

Thirtieth Sunday of the Year

ing by. When some people tried to quiet him, he shouted all the louder, "Son of David, have pity on me!" At the moment he could think of nothing except the possibility that Jesus would cure him. And Jesus did so. In time of great need, Bartimaeus turned to Jesus, but one has to wonder what happened after his cure. Did his appreciation slowly erode after he was freed from blindness, as did that of his ancestors after they had been delivered from exile? We do not know. We have no further record of this man in the gospel, no indication that he was one of the few who became faithful followers of Jesus. Considering human nature, the odds are pretty heavy that after he got what he wanted, he forgot all about Jesus.

Human Nature

I think we will all admit that when we are in deep trouble, when we really need help, we turn almost instinctively to God for help. Such prayer is a good thing, but why do we find it so hard to remember to express our gratitude to God? Here is a simple example. Many Catholic families would never think of beginning a meal without first saying grace, but they frequently forget to say "thanks" after eating. There are reasons of course—the little kids want to watch TV, the teenagers are in a hurry because of a date, the adults linger over their coffee. That's all true, but even in this comparatively small matter we should be conscious of the need to thank God. Why do we fail? Maybe one reason is that we have the idea that prayer is primarily asking God for things we need. Prayer means much more than that. It includes praising God for his goodness and power, and thanking him for extending that goodness and power to us.

Great Things

Maybe the reason we do not thank God the way we should goes deeper than mere forgetfulness or even a failure

BREAKING THE BREAD

to realize that prayer includes thanksgiving. Deep down we may just feel that there is actually precious little to be grateful for. Life is hard—trying to make a marriage happy, doing your best to raise kids when modern circumstances seem to be so much against you, working to make financial ends meet when those ends are miles apart, and wondering whether it is all worth it. We can develop a form of myopia, a spiritual nearsightedness, as we see only present problems under our noses and fail to focus on all the wonderful things God has already done for us and promises us in the future. God is the source of life itself, our creator; he has filled us with every blessing through his son, Jesus Christ, who has saved us from the slavery of sin; God calls us to the joyful vision of his light in heaven (cf. Preface, Fourth Eucharistic Prayer).

Faith

Today in the Fourth Eucharistic Prayer we will recall the wonderful things God has done for us. It is a long list, going back to the beginning of time and reaching out into an era without end. Creation—salvation—eternal life—these are indeed great things for which to be grateful, but they seem so distant, so fuzzy, almost unreal. Yes, our problem is spiritual myopia. If we want to ask for something in prayer, we should ask Jesus to clear up our spiritual vision, as he cured Bartimaeus of his physical blindness. Faith is the only cure for spiritual nearsightedness, a deep faith which enables us to see clearly the truth of today's responsorial psalm: "The Lord has done great things for us."

The suggestion that we pray for faith may seem simple, almost commonplace. Yet there is no cure other than faith. Without real faith we will see religion as if it were a child's balloon, which is brightly colored on the outside, filled only with air on the inside, and which the prick of human problems can easily pop. With faith we can see through externals

Thirtieth Sunday of the Year

and realize that the balloon is filled with the power and goodness of God, and that the balloon will constantly expand without ever bursting. How we must pray for faith! Only with faith can we appreciate the fact that prayer means more than asking for favors. Only with faith can we see clearly that the "Lord has done great things for us," and that we have profound reasons to praise and thank him for his power and love.

C. E. M.

Solemnity of All Saints

THE SAINTS GO MARCHING OUT?*

On a Sunday afternoon eighty thousand people are seated in an arena which resembles the ancient Roman Colosseum. They rise to their feet, and with great gusto sing out, "... the saints come marching in...." Onto the field trot a number of men who resemble the Roman gladiators more than they do the saints who met a martyr's death centuries ago. They are members of the New Orleans Saints, a professional football team.

De-Emphasis

With the recent reduction of saints' days in the Church's calendar, it may seem to some that soon the only thing the word "saints" will suggest is a struggle between two teams in the N.F.L. Recent liturgical reform has indeed de-emphasized saints' days, but it has done so only in order to restore the mystery of Christ as the center of liturgical celebration. This is as it should be. But though saints' days have been "played down," they will continue to form part of the liturgical year and we will continue to celebrate today's feast of All Saints. The real question is not why saints' days have been de-emphasized, but rather why they should be celebrated at all.

* This homily is taken from my article on the subject in *The Homiletic and Pastoral Review* for January, 1970, pp. 271ff.

Solemnity of All Saints

Reason for Continuance

Actually the reason for the continuance of saints' days is precisely the fact that Christ is the center of all liturgical celebration. We must remember that Christ is present and active in the world in many ways. He continues not only in the Eucharist, not only in the words of Sacred Scripture, but also in people. All Christians are called to continue the life of Christ. In the second reading today we were told that we are God's children. As children of God we are like God's child by excellence, God's unique son, Jesus Christ. Through baptism we were given a participation in the life of Christ.

It is not that we are called merely to imitate Christ, as a modern president of the United States may try to imitate, say, Abraham Lincoln. Lincoln is dead. He cannot communicate anything of himself to the living. But Jesus is very much alive, and he does communicate his life to people. Every person in union with Christ by faith and baptism continues his presence in the world. Jesus lived the perfect human life, and his followers continue that life in varying degrees. Some people have lived the Christ-life in an eminent degree. They are the people we call saints.

Meaning of Saints

In the early Church the first saints to be honored were the martyrs. The Church saw that martyrs were conformed to Christ most specially and heroically in dying as he did. When persecutions ended, the Church broadened its vision of how people live the Christ-life. Every Christian death, even though not heroic, is a conformity to Christ in his death. Moreover, all the aspects of the Christ-life are lived out by Christians: his preaching, his healing ministry to the sick, his love and concern for all classes of people, his devotion to children, his intense life of prayer. Saints tend to "specialize"

BREAKING THE BREAD

in reliving certain aspects of the life of Christ. In a St. Vincent de Paul we feel Christ's concern for the poor. In a St. John Chrysostom we hear Christ the great preacher. In a St. Teresa of Avila we see Christ once again spending whole nights in prayer. And today we honor those many unnamed saints, those little people like you and me, who through all the ordinary chores and pleasures of life tried to let Christ and his love radiate from their lives.

How to Celebrate

Today we honor Christ in his saints. We should praise God whose power is so great that he has made the wonderful life of his son continue among us in human persons, and we should thank him for this tremendous favor. We should also pray that we may cooperate with his grace which can make saints of us too. And finally we should ask pardon for our failures in not letting the life of Christ take over our own being.

The saints are not marching out. On the contrary, we can with appreciation, joy, and even gusto, see them come marching into the liturgy as another way of celebrating the great central mystery of Jesus Christ.

C. E. M.

Thirty-First Sunday of the Year
Suggested Use: **Fourth Eucharistic Prayer**

*HEART SPEAKS TO HEART**

A five-year-old girl has been mischievous and disobedient most of the day. As her mother was putting her to bed, she noticed tears in her daughter's eyes and asked, "What is the matter?" The girl replied, "Nobody said he loved me today." The mother smiled and said, "Honey, that's not true. Don't you remember that daddy told you to eat your vegetables at dinner? That was his way of saying that he loves you." The language of the heart has its own vocabulary, but all too often we miss the message. And that is tragic, because unless we hear and understand the language of the heart, the language of love, we cannot love in return. We love those who we know love us.

Something Special

Sometimes something special has to happen to tune us in to the language of the heart. A young man of seventeen was so unhappy that he decided to leave home and live on his own. He moved away and took his own apartment. He soon became miserable in his loneliness, but he feared his father would not accept him back. He called his father on the phone and said: "Dad, don't say anything. I want to come home but I'm afraid. Tomorrow I will be on the bus that passes in back of our orchard. If you want me back, tie a rag to the branch of one of the trees. If I see the rag, I will get off at the depot. If not, I will just keep going." And he hung up before his father could respond. The next day the boy

---

* John Henry Newman's motto as a Cardinal, *Cor Ad Cor Loquitur*.

was on the bus. As he drew closer to home, he realized that he would not have the courage to look for the rag on the tree. There was an old man sitting next to him, and he explained the situation to him. He asked the old man, "Please look for the rag and let me know what you see." As they passed the orchard, the old man said nothing but started to sob. The boy thought all was lost. "No rag on the tree?" he asked. The old man turned slowly in his seat and said, "Young man, your father had a rag tied to every tree in that orchard." —The love of the father was not something new, but the son had failed to hear the language of the heart and so had failed to love in return.

God's Language of Love

The message of today's Mass is that we must love God with our whole being and let this love overflow in our love for our fellow men. But we are not moved to this kind of love if we do not know that God loves us. God's love surrounds us in the past, in the present, and in the future. And yet how easy it is to miss his language of love. The language of his heart is made up not primarily of words but of deeds. That is what we will profess in the Fourth Eucharistic Prayer: "Father, we acknowledge your greatness: all your *actions* show your wisdom and love." God is a loving Father who has created us and called us to be his children. As a Father he has love for us. We should feel his concern in the air we breathe, in the food we eat, in the whole earth upon which we live. We should sense his kindness in every new dawn, his gentleness in every breeze, and his care in every restful night. We should see his goodness shining through the eyes of those we love. As his children we await an eternal inheritance.

God's Special Sign

Above all we must never forget that something special has happened to tune us in to the language of God's heart. God

Thirty-First Sunday of the Year

did not tie a rag to a tree in an orchard as a sign of his love. Instead he has lifted up his own son on the tree of the cross. "God so loved the world that he gave his only son." We just cannot find a greater sign of love than that. But God is not satisfied with leaving that great sign of love lost in the past of history. So that we won't forget, he renews the sacrifice of his son for us as a living reality in every Mass we celebrate. God's heart speaks to our heart if we only listen.

C. E. M.

Thirty-Second Sunday of the Year
Suggested Use: Third Eucharistic Prayer

THE WIDOW'S MITE

Jesus praised the poor widow who put only two small coins into the collection box of the temple because she gave all she had. We can quite readily identify with the reaction of Jesus since most of us have, in one way or another, had the same reaction. It is the joy in the heart of a mother when her four-year-old daughter presents her with a dandelion and sincerely says, "A pretty flower for you, Mom." A splendid bouquet could not satisfy her more. It is the pride felt by a father when his young son earnestly says, "Gee, dad, you can really throw that football." Being named the most valuable player in the N.F.L. could not please him more.

Giving, Not Receiving

Yes, most of us at some time have received a gift or a word of praise, small or insignificant in itself, which has taken on a special value, a preciousness, in our eyes. The value was derived, not from what was given, but from the sincerity and earnestness of the giver. Today, however, we should think about whether we have been the giver in a similar situation—whether we have been like the widow in her relationship with God. I am not talking about putting money into the collection basket, important though that be. Money is necessary for the support of your parish and its many activities, but there is something more vital. God wants not only our generosity in giving money. He wants our generosity in giving ourselves.

Giving Ourselves

I think that as Catholics we have often heard the idea that we should offer ourselves to God in the Mass, that we

Thirty-Second Sunday of the Year

should make a gift of all that we have done, as well as all our joys and sorrows, together with a promise to try to lead a life in the future worthy of giving to God. The gift of ourselves is an act of love and praise of God. How valuable, however, is our gift? We may feel that its intrinsic worth is not much more than that of a dandelion from a little girl or a word of praise from a small boy. We know that sincerity and earnestness are important, but are even they sufficient to transform our offering into something truly significant to God? Actually within the Mass our lives can take on a whole new value.

Catholic doctrine teaches us that within the Mass Jesus renews the offering of himself on the cross, the gift of himself to his Father. The death of Jesus was the most excellent act of love and praise the world has ever known. It was an act truly worthy of God the Father. Nothing that has happened on this earth has pleased and satisfied God more. But where do we come in? Through the Mass Jesus makes the offering of himself to the Father a *living* sacrifice, so that his offering becomes the Church's offering, *our* offering.* Notice what happens at Mass: during the Preparation of the Gifts at the altar a drop of water is placed in the chalice. That drop of water mingles with the wine and becomes part of it. The tiny, almost worthless drop of water now shares in the nature of wine as it takes on its color and flavor. In somewhat the same way Jesus takes our human lives and transforms them in the Mass so that they become a part of his sacrifice. Jesus renews the offering of himself in the Mass, not for his sake, but for ours so that he may catch up our ordinary human joys and sorrows, our work and our play, and give them a new, extraordinary meaning.

---

* Cf. the words of the Third Eucharistic Prayer following the consecration: "We offer you in thanksgiving this holy and living sacrifice. Look with favor on your Church's offering...."

BREAKING THE BREAD

Real Value

The entire Eucharistic Prayer is an act of worship of God, but it is particularly at the time of the consecration that Jesus makes himself present as a victim of sacrifice. During those moments you should not be merely passive spectators. You should be aware of the fact that something is happening—that Jesus is renewing the offering of himself to the Father and he is inviting you to offer yourselves with him. The expression of that offering reaches its culmination in the great doxology: "Through him, with him, in him, in the unity of the Holy Spirit, all glory and honor is yours, almighty Father, for ever and ever." Your strong and fervent "Amen" is your way of proclaiming in one word that you share with Christ the offering of himself in praise and love for the Father.°°

The point is that we can do something very worthwhile here at Mass. The two coins which the widow put into the collection box of the temple pleased God because of her sincerity and generosity, but all the sincerity and generosity in the world could not make those two coins actually worth more than their face value. Our offering in the Mass needs

---

°° "Let the faithful consider to what a high dignity they are raised by the sacrament of baptism. They should not think it enough to participate in the Eucharistic Sacrifice with that general intention which befits members of Christ and children of the Church, but let them further, in keeping with the spirit of the sacred liturgy, be most closely united with the High Priest and his earthly minister, at the time the consecration of the divine Victim is effected, and at that time especially when those solemn words are pronounced, 'Through him, with him, in him,' etc. To these words in fact the people answer 'Amen.' Nor should Christians forget to offer themselves, their cares, their sorrows, their distress and their necessities in union with their Divine Savior upon the Cross" (*Mediator Dei*, 104).

Thirty-Second Sunday of the Year

our sincerity and generosity to make it pleasing to God, but Jesus himself gives our offering a real value which it could never have by itself.

C. E. M.

Thirty-Third Sunday of the Year

LIFE AFTER DEATH: THAT'S PROGRESS

November is a strange time of year. Trees have finally lost their leaves. But winter snow hasn't come to the east coast, nor winter rain to the west coast. The holiday bustle has yet to begin. Nights are long. Things are quiet. It's a good time to think about death, which the Church does. And Christ in the Gospel would have us think about the "death" of the world: when the "stars will fall from the skies and the heavenly hosts will be shaken." Okay, let's get down to it. Is it near? When will the end come? Is 1975 the year as some say or the year 2,000?

Fr. Teilhard Suggests

Fr. Teilhard de Chardin, the paleontologist and poet, presents in his writings an outline of the life-to-death of our universe, which might help to think out what the end will be like. Father suggests that at the dawn of creation God provided an original or central source from which matter, plants and life first sprang under his creative force. In the early eons of development living things took on various shapes and forms. There were simply many different kinds of plants and animals and even "pre-men." Once this process was completed and the stage was set, the creation of man as Genesis knows him was achieved. And with man, practically speaking, physical evolution was finished. But a more complex form of God's creation continued: namely, mental-social evolution; or what we might call the "progress" of man. And this progress seemed aimed at bringing unity to the world split with diversity.

Thirty-Third Sunday of the Year

Over the ages of time, man has felt compelled to perfect things, to find ways to move quickly over great distances, to talk to far horizons, to make profoundly different and better mouse traps. It's as though something deep within man in each age has magnetically responded to a pulling force. If you saw the movie "2001" some years back, men were searching for a large slab monolith. In the movie they seemed to be pulled by the magnetic force of this slab. Teilhard asserts that the "itch" man feels to progress, to get better, is simply the "magnetic" force of God's creative love pulling all things to himself the Creator.

Unity in our Times

During recent history, it's apparent that man has almost instinctively been searching for unity, or oneness. Just consider the progress of transportation and communication creating the global village. The formation of the United Nations, the expansion of the Common Market, even the Second Vatican Council are clear examples of man's instinct for unity.

Jesus Christ came to perfect unity through a new commandment: Love. Where love is, there is no disunity, no divided cause. Christ comes with power to remove the one real obstacle to progress: sin. Selfishness, hatred were man's wrench to sabotage the unity and progress of the planet. Yet through his death and resurrection (coming to us in the Sacraments) Christ offered unity and advancement at each step of our life, and each age to come. "Jesus offered the one sacrifice for sins and took his seat forever at the right hand of God. By one offering he has forever perfected those who have been sanctified." Christ continues to offer the power to perfect progress.

Vital Conclusions

We can draw conclusions from this sketchy Teilhard picture. First of all, quite happily we seem close to the last days. At least the scene is better organized. As the *Pax Romana* was the era necessary for Christ's first coming, our technological unity of today may be sufficient for the second coming. And then, if we want to hurry the progress of unity (returning to the Father and the second coming of Christ) we have to take down barriers of distrust and suspicion in all areas: in politics, schools, at home. In God's plan of creation there are not two separated areas: spirit vs. material. There is a blessed unity of spirit helping material bodies to move faster, of Christ helping the world progress to the resurrection. This very Mass we celebrate unleashes more power to unify all of us: to be one in faith and love, in the Greeting of Peace, in the Body of Christ. We can hasten the progress of our day more quickly to the final evolution of our world: the resurrection and unity with God.

Next week we proclaim Christ as King. This is no empty title. Christ is and will be King of all ages, all progress in all areas. Lord, you show us the path to life, fullness of joys in your presence and the delights at your right hand forever. In the light of the Resurrection, death simply is the next step in God's plan of creation. And the final "death" of the world will be the final turnover to the eternal spring.

M. M. R.

Thirty-Fourth and Last Sunday of the Year
Solemnity of Christ the King

THE KING AND HIS NOBLES

To say that Jesus is a King does not mean a whole lot to us these days. Our ideas of a king, surrounded by his court of nobles, are rather jumbled and confused, a conglomerate from historical data, fairy tales, and old Disney movies. Even the people of our Lord's own day did not have very clear ideas, because they compared Jesus and his kingdom with their own human experience. It was somewhat like comparing a Boeing 747 with the simple airplane flown by the Wright brothers at Kitty Hawk back in 1903. The people had to make a tremendous jump in their thinking before they could begin to understand what Jesus really intended.

In today's gospel episode Jesus recognized that Pilate had failed to make that jump. "Are you the King of the Jews?" Pilate asked, and he was thinking only of a type of person who was a military and political leader, a man who could possibly be a threat to Roman authority in Palestine. "My kingdom does not belong to this world," Jesus replied, and he meant that he was not the kind of king Pilate imagined, not a ruler whose followers would fight for him as soldiers in a war or whose domain was limited to one nation.

The Kingdom

Of course Jesus does have a domain. It is a universal kingdom, for Jesus has authority over all creation. This domain is well described in today's preface: "a kingdom of truth and life, a kingdom of holiness and grace, a kingdom of justice, love, and peace." That certainly sounds like a fitting kingdom for Jesus Christ, but it also sounds very ideal and quite futuristic with a reality only in heaven. To some extent this evaluation is correct. The perfect kingdom is yet to come, and we are the people who "wait in joyful hope for the coming of our Savior, Jesus Christ." Jesus will come again when the world is at an end. The end of the world, however, does not mean catastrophe but fulfillment. To say that a house or building is finished and the work ended does not imply destruction but perfection. That is the kind of end to which our world, and indeed the whole universe, will be brought.

Development

Right now the condition of the kingdom is similar to that of a child who has a lot of developing to do before he becomes a mature man, grown to full stature in the prime of life. Christ will come to claim his kingdom and present it to the Father when its perfection in the divine plan has been reached. Meanwhile, we are not to just sit around and hope that our King will get this work done all by himself. Though all of creation is Christ's kingdom, we are very important members of that kingdom. Not one of us is a mere pawn or peasant; we are all nobles, "a people set apart, a chosen race, a royal priesthood." We are called to be close cooperators with the king in making the kingdom reach its ideal. We should not expect Christ to replace our present world with some kind of prefabricated paradise. We ourselves have to work for a better world, prepared and fit to come fully under God's dominion as a kingdom of justice, love, and peace.*

Enthusiasm

Though we have to be realistic about the many imperfections of our world and our society, it is unchristian to be

---

* Cf. *Pastoral Constitution on the Church in the Modern World*, paragraph 39.

Thirty-Fourth Sunday of the Year

pessimistic and tragic to be apathetic. The Catholic who does nothing to better world conditions is a scandalous cop-out. The present time should be one of tremendous dynamism, hope, and enthusiasm. But where do we start? For one thing, we should see that, since Christ has dominion over all of creation, the ecological movement, though fraught with complications, is fundamentally Christian. We should be active in ecological programs with a Christian perspective that God has put the resources of this world into our hands to be used properly, not abused for greedy and selfish purposes. Part of this perspective is the truth that the earth and all its resources are intended by the Creator to help people fulfill their destiny, and that, to put it bluntly, the welfare of human beings is more important than preserving some endangered species of alligator in Florida or condors in California.

Love and Peace

Ecology, moreover, is not our greatest problem. Because Christ's kingdom is to be one of justice, love, and peace, the biggest obstacles to its growth toward perfection are injustice, hatred, and war. These seem to be such momentous evils that one wonders what a single person can do. We must remember that if everyone thought he was powerless, then indeed nothing would ever be accomplished. You may feel that there is nothing you can do to overcome the grave injustices in this world or the inequities of wealth, but in your own life you can try to respect all human beings without exception, and you can be more generous and unselfish with the material goods God has given you. You may not be able to put a stop to war, but war is in reality the worst expansion of hatred between individuals. What you can do is to work for love and peace within your own home and with the people you see everyday. Our sign of peace in the Mass is

BREAKING THE BREAD

a simple reminder that Christ calls us to spread his kingdom and love to the whole world. We can indeed make a beginning with those who are close to us, but it is only a beginning. Rather than being satisfied with a limited sphere of influence, we should be constantly searching for ways to inject Christian principles into our world and to correct the abuses of our society.

Nobles

Jesus is a king who wishes to conquer the world, not through war or by means of trampling on the rights of others. Rather he wants to bring peace and happiness through justice and love. He has entrusted the spreading of his kingdom to us, the nobles of his court. He could do it all himself, but he wants us to work with him in bringing the world to fulfillment. We wait in joyful hope for the coming of our Savior Jesus Christ. But right now our labors for a better world give meaning to our words addressed to Christ the King: "The kingdom, the power, and the glory are yours now and forever."

C. E. M.